HAIR

THE STORY OF THE SHOW
THAT DEFINED A GENERATION

Eric Grode
Foreword by James Rado

RUNNING
PRESS

To Beth and Jonathan,
the sources of so many
singing songs

RIGHT An issue of the
Playbill for *HAIR*, with
improvisatory sketchwork
by Gerome Ragni, and
signed "Love Jerry" for
Dagmar, *HAIR*'s original
official photographer.

© 2010 by Eric Grode (text)
© 2010 by Carlton Books Ltd (design)
HAIR is licensed by Aquarius Broadway LLC in
association with The Public Theater, Jeffrey
Richards, and Jerry Frankel

All rights reserved under the Pan-American and
International Copyright Conventions

Printed in Dubai

9 8 7 6 5 4 3 2 1

Digit on the right indicates the number of this
printing

Library of Congress Control Number: 2010928628

ISBN 978-0-7624-4128-0

Running Press Book Publishers
2300 Chestnut Street
Philadelphia, PA 19103-4371

Visit us on the web!
www.runningpress.com

CONTENTS

FOREWORD

A black plume of burning oil rises from the Gulf of Mexico, a volcano has erupted in Iceland; one a man–made environmental disaster, one a phenomenon of nature. Someone in a question–answer session asked recently: "Mr. Rado, what supernatural vortex were you and Gerome in when you wrote *HAIR*?" Which brought back to my mind that we did talk about the feeling of the "V" (vortex,) that we were being communicated to from on high; we became aware of the "collective unconscious," as a psychic friend of ours tried to explain what was happening to us. The truth is we unlocked each other, Gerome (Jerry) and I. He was my creative catalyst, I probably his. We found a subject to dramatize, something that was happening around us that we could enter into, a new world that took root before our eyes and manifested in all its glory for us to taste, smell, see, hear, touch, smoke. Although we wrote the play before we had ever smoked, at a certain point, the leaves of "marijane" did come into play. I was more or less a confirmed teetotaler, but came to like the forbidden weed, once I learned how to cope with its paranoia-producing initial effect. The paranoia came from the guilt of breaking away from the society of the country we had loved and were part of. But we felt like true patriots, because we did believe in the ideas of freedom and liberty and love-thy-neighbor which were the good parts that had been instilled in us. But the hippies took it even further. They brought us to a world of greater freedom that tested freedom, that made us know freedom was an important thing to aspire to. The hippies were earthy and beautiful, some of them barefoot on city sidewalks, with a new openness. They talked about infinity, and they talked about the nowness of now with newness. Jerry and I infiltrated them, grew our hair long, and Jerry discovered and saw for the first time his own heady crop. We two thespians wrote and wrote and made a script that fell into the hands of Joseph Papp. The rest is history and I am pleased it has been compiled in this book.

JAMES RADO

LEFT *HAIR*'s three creators: James Rado (left,) Galt MacDermot (top,) and Gerome Ragni (right.)

RIGHT A leaflet for the Munich, Germany, production signed by Rado.

ABOVE An audience leaflet for *HAIR* in the style of a tarot card. The original production *HAIR* actually had its own company card reader, Earl Scott.

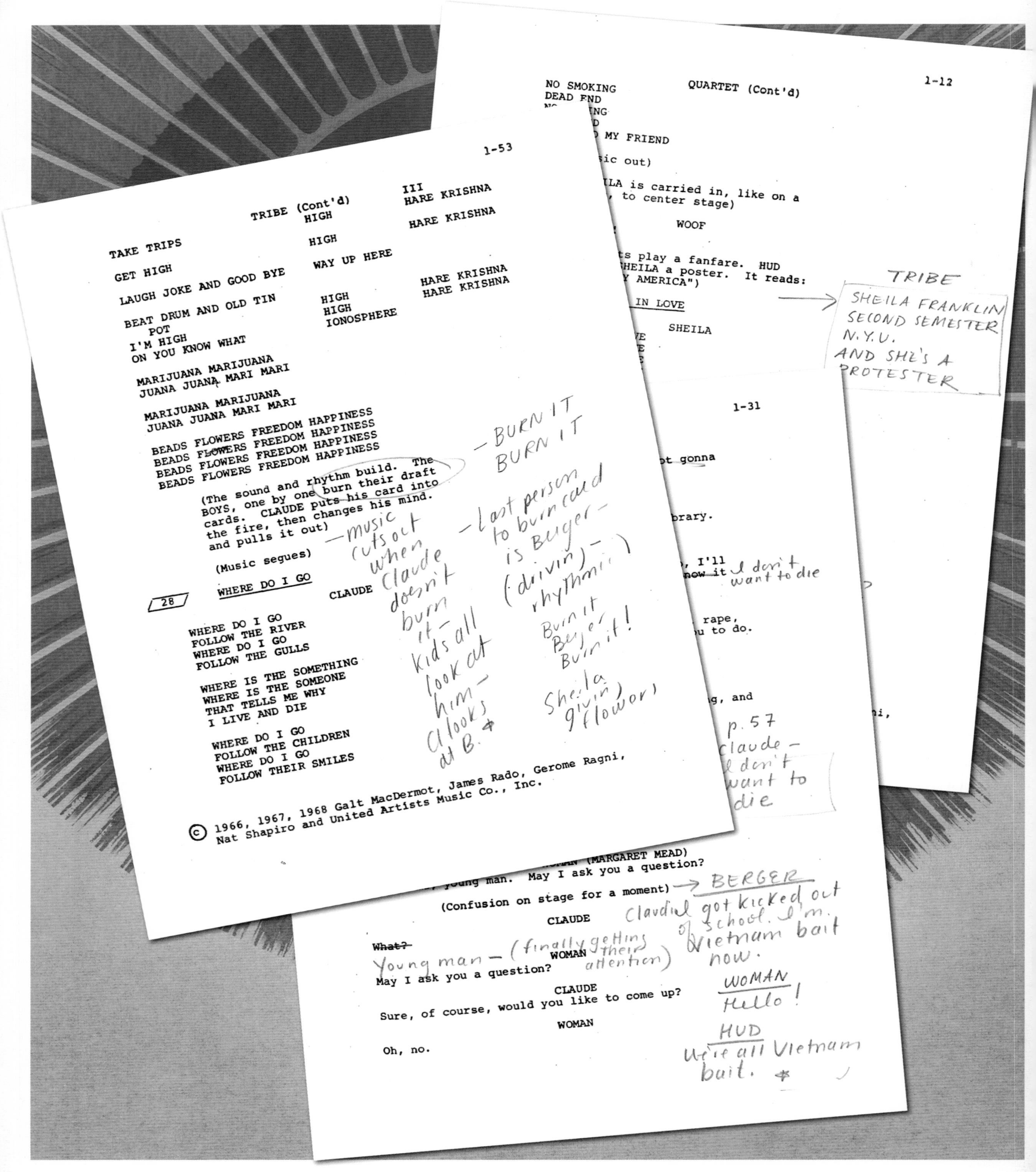

1-53

TRIBE (Cont'd)

TAKE TRIPS | HIGH | III HARE KRISHNA
GET HIGH | HIGH | HARE KRISHNA
LAUGH JOKE AND GOOD BYE | WAY UP HERE |
BEAT DRUM AND OLD TIN POT | HIGH HIGH IONOSPHERE | HARE KRISHNA HARE KRISHNA
I'M HIGH
ON YOU KNOW WHAT

MARIJUANA MARIJUANA
JUANA JUANA MARI MARI

MARIJUANA MARIJUANA
JUANA JUANA MARI MARI

BEADS FLOWERS FREEDOM HAPPINESS
BEADS FLOWERS FREEDOM HAPPINESS
BEADS FLOWERS FREEDOM HAPPINESS
BEADS FLOWERS FREEDOM HAPPINESS

(The sound and rhythm build. The BOYS, one by one burn their draft cards. CLAUDE puts his card into the fire, then changes his mind and pulls it out)

(Music segues)

28 WHERE DO I GO

CLAUDE

WHERE DO I GO
FOLLOW THE RIVER
WHERE DO I GO
FOLLOW THE GULLS

WHERE IS THE SOMETHING
WHERE IS THE SOMEONE
THAT TELLS ME WHY
I LIVE AND DIE

WHERE DO I GO
FOLLOW THE CHILDREN
WHERE DO I GO
FOLLOW THEIR SMILES

—BURN IT BURN IT
—music cuts out when Claude doesn't burn it—kids all look at him—Cl looks at B.
—Last person to burn card is Berger—(drivin) rhythmic
Burn it Berger Burn it!
Sheila givin flowers

NO SMOKING | QUARTET (Cont'd) | 1-12
DEAD END
MY FRIEND
sic out)
ILA is carried in, like on a
, to center stage)
WOOF
ts play a fanfare. HUD
HEILA a poster. It reads:
Y AMERICA")
IN LOVE
SHEILA

TRIBE
SHEILA FRANKLIN
SECOND SEMESTER
N.Y.U.
AND SHE'S A PROTESTER

1-31
ot gonna
brary.
, I'll
now it — I don't want to die
rape,
u to do.
g, and
ni,

p.57
Claude — I don't want to die

WOMAN (MARGARET MEAD)
young man. May I ask you a question?
(Confusion on stage for a moment) → BERGER
Claude got kicked out of school. I'm Vietnam bait now.

CLAUDE
~~What?~~
WOMAN
Young man — (finally getting their attention)
May I ask you a question?
CLAUDE
Sure, of course, would you like to come up?
WOMAN
Oh, no.

WOMAN
Hello!
HUD
We're all Vietnam bait.

INTRODUCTION

"The impassioned plea of today's young people." "Cheap, foul-mouthed, vulgar, and tasteless." The first rock musical. The first concept musical. The death of Broadway. The future of Broadway.

These and many other descriptions have been lobbed at *HAIR*, the first real attempt to explain and extoll the hippie subculture to mainstream America, since it debuted in New York's East Village in 1967. And while the "American Tribal Love-Rock Musical," as it was subtitled has become all but synonymous with hippiedom for tens of millions of people, the story of its creation—one that would include titans of the period's experimental theater scene as well as wide-eyed teenagers, and shrewd business calculations as well as touching displays of optimism—has largely been forgotten.

In its absence, a dizzying set of narratives and counter-narratives have flooded in to make an already complicated story even more so. Tales of backstage debauchery jostle with misty-eyed paeans to an innocence and activism that has now been lost forever.

Both of these threads play a significant role in the story of *HAIR*, along with many others, and it is the goal of this book—the first authorized history of the show, from its origins in Hoboken, New Jersey, and Chicago to the acclaimed 2009 Broadway revival—to contextualize as well as address them. In doing so, I have relied heavily on the reminiscences of dozens of people involved with the various productions, from its creators to backstage personnel to original tribe members to one of the *Apollo 13* astronauts who walked out of a performance. Each of these men and women was patient and courteous in handling a barrage of questions, and I am grateful to them all.

Words make up only one part of what this book has to offer. Extremely rare photos and documents, many of them never published before, capture this rhapsodic, roiling period better than any description can. And the lyrics by James Rado and Gerome Ragni—sprawling and often goofy yet incisive, firmly rooted in their era yet utterly timeless—offer the most pointed glimpse into the inspired and inspiring world of *HAIR*. Thanks to these words and the myriad actors, musicians, directors, and designers who have helped give voice to them, the Age of Aquarius continues to dawn anew for audiences around the world.

ERIC GRODE

LEFT Excerpts from the script for the 2009 Broadway revival, complete with annotations by director Diane Paulus.

TOP Diane Keaton and Emmeretta Marks in the original Broadway production.

ABOVE The original Broadway cast on stage.

THE HIPPIES

Decades rarely lend themselves to the kind of tidy sorting that so many people try to apply to them after the fact, and the 1960s are no exception. However, a number of seminal events did indeed take place in 1960, their consequences playing a potent role in defining the world that the tribe in *HAIR* alternately rages against and embraces. Several themes that course through *HAIR* touch upon these events, from race (a series of sit-ins in segregated Southern U.S. businesses attracted worldwide attention to the burgeoning civil rights movement) to sexual liberation (the U.S. authorities approved usage of Enovid, better known as "the Pill," as an oral contraceptive) to the possibilities of youth (John F. Kennedy, at 43, became the youngest man elected U.S. president) to popular music (an English rock band known as The Quarrymen began a 48-night gig in Hamburg, Germany, and changed its name to The Beatles.)

TOP Teenagers in Birmingham, Alabama, take part in a civil rights march in May 1963. The march, which included more than 1,000 students, would end with high-pressure water hoses and police dogs.

LEFT President John F. Kennedy makes his inauguration speech from the balcony of the White House on January 20, 1961.

ABOVE Beatlemania was in full swing in the United States by 1964. Performing here are, from left, Paul McCartney, George Harrison, and John Lennon.

RIGHT In 1965, policemen struggle to restrain screaming teenagers at the hotel where The Beatles were staying in New York City before their legendary Shea Stadium concert.

ABOVE Jack Kerouac in 1957, the year that his pioneering book *On the Road* was published.

LEFT A massive crowd marches from New York's Central Park toward United Nations Plaza as part of an anti-Vietnam War demonstration on April 15, 1967.

However, the roots of the hippie movement as well as those of the world event that played as large a role as any in crystallizing it—the Vietnam War— go deeper still.

James Rado doesn't remember the exact date when he and Gerome Ragni borrowed a typewriter from their landlord in Hoboken, New Jersey and wrote "White Boys/Black Boys." However, *HAIR* was already in the works when the two men appeared together in Mike Nichols's production of the hit play *The Knack* in Chicago in 1965. Therefore it is all but certain that they were writing about hippies before hippies even existed—at least by that name. The word was coined by a San Francisco newspaper columnist on September 5, 1965; the title of his article, "A New Haven for Beatniks," gives an indication of what these scruffy young men and women had been called up until then.

The beatniks, who came into prominence in the late 1940s, shared many of the same anti-authoritarian beliefs as their successors. The hippies shied away from standard Judeo-Christian beliefs in favor of Eastern mysticism; *über*-beatnik Jack Kerouac wrote a *roman à clef* called *The Dharma Bums* (1958.) The hippies defined themselves in opposition to the government and other authority figures; the beatniks often espoused libertarian beliefs. The hippies promulgated the expansion of consciousness through controlled substances; the beatniks swore by *The Doors of Perception* (1954.) Aldous Huxley's account of taking the hallucinogenic drug mescaline. Kerouac's subsequent definition of the beatnik philosophy could be used almost verbatim to describe hippies: "a generation of crazy, illuminated hipsters suddenly rising and roaming America, serious, bumming and hitchhiking everywhere, ragged, beatific, beautiful in an ugly graceful new way."

However, the buildup of the Cold War provided a useful set of criteria by which the hippie movement could set itself apart. The proliferation of nuclear weapons lent an added sense of urgency to the hippies' insistence on peace and harmony. More important, the Vietnam War, which escalated as a direct result of the Cold War-era "domino theory" that warned against allowing the spread of Communism anywhere in the world, confirmed many of their attitudes in opposition to what they called the Establishment.

What we think of as the hippie movement began in Berkeley, California, where a few dozen *habitués* of the Cabale Creamery, a prominent folk-music coffee house, attended an all-night Native American peyote ceremony. This group would ultimately establish a sort of synthesis between folk music and the emerging genre of psychedelic rock, convening a mix of music, light shows, and other sorts of psychedelic experiments at the Red Dog Saloon in Virginia City, an isolated mining town in Nevada. Jefferson Airplane, the Grateful Dead, and Big Brother and the Holding Company were just some of the bands who became part of what was soon known as "the Red Dog Experience."

The members of this community soon gravitated toward the Haight-Ashbury district of San Francisco, and some 15,000 like-minded men and women—the original "hippies"—had joined them there by the summer of 1966. LSD (the hallucinogenic drug lysergic acid diethylamide) had not yet been deemed a controlled substance in California, and psychedelic drugs soon became a crucial part of the culture. Free drugs was just one of the services provided by the Diggers, a street-theater troupe that organized free concerts, gave out free food (sometimes at "free stores" that had no prices,) and performed impromptu works of anarchic

street theater. When James Rado talked to a *New York Times* reporter in 1967 during rehearsals at Joseph Papp's Public Theater (where *HAIR* would begin its tumultuous journey,) the troupe was clearly on his mind. "You know, the Diggers just opened a new free store in the East Village," Rado said. "Joe Papp has been doing it for years."

The location of the Public, on the edge of the East Village, Manhattan, had a lot to do with that statement. Ten thousand people, many but by no means all of them hippies, had gathered in Central Park on Easter Sunday of 1967 for what was called a "Be-In," kicking off a period that became known as the Summer of Love. New York's hippies were rarely spotted this far north, though, as Greenwich Village became the locus of the movement on the East Coast. This would prove convenient when costume designer Theoni V. Aldredge found herself at a loss during preproduction for *HAIR* at the Public. "Theoni had no clue what hippies looked like," says Amy Saltz, who was assisting the show's director, Gerald Freedman. "I would go over to St. Mark's Place and take pictures and give them to her."

She might have also gotten some assistance from "The Hippies: The Philosophy of a Subculture," a cover story that ran in *Time* magazine just a few weeks earlier, in July 1967. Its distillation of the hippie credo read in part, "Blow the mind of every straight person you can reach. Turn them on, if not to drugs, then to beauty, love, honesty, fun." ("Straight" in this context referred to membership in the perceived Establishment as opposed to sexual orientation.) It was during this summer that about 100,000 more people came to San Francisco to join the scene.

ALLEN GINSBERG

The song "Three-Five-Zero-Zero" contains many cryptic allusions to war, and an instructive (though by no means complete) guide can be found in the works of Allen Ginsberg, a pivotal figure of what became known as the Beat Generation. Best known for the poems "Howl" (1956) and "Kaddish" (1959) and for his depiction in Jack Kerouac's *On the Road* under the alias Carlo Marx, Ginsberg (seen here at a 1965 "mass reading" in London) was a prominent proponent of Krishnaism and a vocal protester against the Vietnam War. He and Ken Kesey were believed to have played a crucial role in defusing tension between thousands of antiwar marchers and the Hell's Angels before a 1965 march on the Oakland–Berkeley city line in California.

The material in question can be found in Ginsberg's 1966 poem "Wichita Vortex Sutra," which the poet recorded on a handheld tape recorder as he spent three months traveling cross country in a Volkswagen bus. (He had asked Bob Dylan for enough money to buy a tape machine.) Ginsberg hypothesizes that the conservatism of Middle America—exemplified by Wichita, Kansas, where the hatchet-wielding Carry Nation waged her war on alcohol—led directly to the Vietnam War. Or, as he put it, Wichita "began a vortex of hatred that defoliated the Mekong Delta."

"Three-Five-Zero-Zero" uses several chunks of the poem intact ("Caught in barbed wire / Fireball / Bullet shock") and paraphrases other parts (Ginsberg's "The war is over now / Except for the souls / held prisoner in Niggertown" became "Prisoners in Niggertown / It's a dirty little war.") The first five words of the song can be found in the second half of this line, which brings the reader to the Wichita setting: "flesh soft as a Kansas girl's / ripped open by metal explosion."

The title, meanwhile, has generated some confusion. It comes from a passage in which U.S. General Maxwell Taylor refers to "Vietcong losses leveling up three five zero zero per month," although 3,800 appears to be the actual number. The U.S. Marines who landed at Da Nang in 1965, officially shifting American involvement in Vietnam from a nominally advisory role to one of active combat, also numbered 3,500, and many have assumed that this was the source of the title.

Incidentally, Ginsberg—who collaborated with Philip Glass in the 1980s on setting "Wichita Vortex Sutra" and some of his other poems to music—did not give permission to have his words used in *HAIR*. Galt MacDermot learned of this years later from Ginsberg himself. "I was doing a concert at some church, and Philip Glass and Allen Ginsberg had an act going. Ginsberg said to me, 'You took my lyric for *HAIR*.' I had no idea! I said, 'No, Jim and Jerry gave me the lyric.'"

THREE-FIVE-ZERO-ZERO

Ripped open by metal explosion
Caught in barbed wire
Fireball
Bullet shock
Bayonet
Electricity
Shrapnel
Throbbing meat
Electronic data processing
Black uniforms
Bare feet, carbines
Mail-order rifles
Shoot the muscles
256 Viet Cong captured
256 Viet Cong captured

Prisoners in Niggertown
It's a dirty little war
Three Five Zero Zero
Take weapons up and begin to kill
Watch the long long armies drifting home

WALKING IN SPACE

Doors locked (doors locked)
Blinds pulled (blinds pulled)
Lights low (lights low)
Flames high (flames high)

My body (my body)
My body

My body (my body)
My body

My body
Is walking in space
My soul is in orbit
With God face to face

Floating, flipping
Flying, tripping

Tripping from Potsville to Mainline
Tripping from Mainline to Moonville

(Tripping from Potsville to Starlight
Tripping from Starlight to Moonville)

On a rocket to
The Fourth Dimension
Total self awareness
The intention

My mind is as clear as country air
I feel my flesh, all colors mesh

Red black
Blue brown

Yellow crimson
Green orange
Purple pink
Violet white
White white
White white
White white

All the clouds are cumuloft
Walking in space
Oh my God your skin is soft
I love your face

How dare they try to end this beauty?
How dare they try to end this beauty?
To keep us under foot
They bury us in soot
Pretending it's a chore
To ship us off to war

In this dive
We rediscover sensation
In this dive
We rediscover sensation

Walking in space
We find the purpose of peace
The beauty of life
You can no longer hide

Our eyes are open
Our eyes are open
Our eyes are open
Our eyes are open
Wide wide wide!

"Three-Five-Zero-Zero"

Starting in a whisper and building to an aggrieved roar, the tribe sings poetically about the horrors of war, with an (uncredited) assist by Allen Ginsberg.

JAMES RADO:: *"I thought that lyric was ours—I didn't know Jerry had borrowed it. But I think it's great that Allen Ginsberg is in there with Shakespeare."*

"Walking in Space"

What starts as a woozy, hallucinogenic-inspired "rocket to the fourth dimension" becomes the first piece in the show's protracted antiwar sequence: "How dare they try to end this beauty?"

GALT MACDERMOT: *"It's a good song. It just goes on—it doesn't stop. There's a lot of interesting writing."*

With this explosion in popularity came the inevitable backlash. Haight-Ashbury didn't have room for all of these migrants, many of them young men and women who found themselves homeless and/or strung out on drugs. Public perception of the hippies had less to do with beauty, love, etc., and more with excess and lassitude, and even the Diggers were prompted to pronounce the "death" of the hippie.

Finally, just as California provided the genesis of the hippie movement, two events in that state in 1969 would see the hippie movement discredited and even reviled in the popular press. First came a series of grisly murders on two consecutive August nights by followers of Charles Manson, who adopted much of the aesthetics but none of the ethos of the hippies; then, four months later, the Altamont Free Concert—touted as "Woodstock West"—resulted in an 18-year-old being stabbed to death by a member of the Hell's Angels motorcycle gang who was working on security detail. Jefferson Airplane, which was part of the "Red Dog Experience" at the beginning, had performed in the concert, but the escalating violence earlier in the day had convinced the Grateful Dead to drop out of their assigned spot.

As the hippie movement was fading, however, the Vietnam War was quickly accelerating. Keith Carradine, who played the hippie and conflicted patriot Claude Bukowski during the Broadway run of *HAIR*, has stated simply that Vietnam was the reason the show existed—and few involved with the show would dispute this. The draft and the counterculture sprouting up in its shadow were what compelled Rado and Ragni to write the show in the first place; growing concern over U.S. involvement in the war drew producer Michael Butler to transfer the show from the Public Theater. While the show subsequently underwent changes that downplayed this aspect of the script somewhat, the specter of a war that would ultimately last eight years continued to hang over not only Claude but the entire tribe.

By the time *HAIR* opened at the Public, the war had officially been going on for almost three years, but tensions had been building in the region formerly known as French Indochina (often owing in part to behind-the-scenes U.S. involvement) since at least 1946, when the United States and the other Western powers agreed to support France in its battle against the Vietnamese Communist forces of Ho Chi Minh. The Geneva Accords of 1954 split the country into North and South Vietnam and dictated that elections be held for the purpose of reunification, but the South Vietnamese president vetoed this proposal in the face of an overwhelming Communist victory.

Initial U.S. efforts were directed toward propping up a "third force" of indigenous Vietnamese leaders opposed to French colonialism as well as Communism, the primary example being Prime Minister Ngo Dinh Diem. President Eisenhower had considered a military escalation in the region as early as 1954, including scenarios that featured the use of tactical nuclear weapons, but it wasn't until an insurgency took root in 1956 among Communist forces in South Vietnam (a group that would become known as the Viet Cong) that the Cold War drumbeat began to intensify.

Three North Vietnamese torpedo boats fired upon a U.S. Navy destroyer in the Gulf of Tonkin in 1964, prompting President Johnson to request permission from Congress to employ additional military power, and the following year would

RIGHT Audience members look on as Hell's Angels beat a fan with pool cues at the Altamont Free Concert, as depicted in the documentary *Gimme Shelter*.

BELOW Gerome Ragni, James Rado's co-author and costar.

OFF-OFF-BROADWAY

RIGHT Like *HAIR*, which opened a year earlier, the rock musical *Your Own Thing* (based on Shakespeare's *Twelfth Night*) drew inspiration from the vibrant off-off-Broadway scene.

Off-off-Broadway as we think of it today only came into existence in the mid-1950s, with the advent of a handful of tiny, adventurous theaters situated below 14th Street in Manhattan. Three theaters from this defiantly downtown scene would ultimately play a direct role in the evolution of *HAIR,* which did as much as any production to introduce mainstream culture to the movement's shambolic, daring, resourceful, often baffling ways.

The most obvious one is the New York Shakespeare Festival, which attained the somewhat more established classification of off-Broadway in 1967 when it unveiled its East Village theater complex with the world premiere of *HAIR*. Prior to that, the Festival, which had begun as an acting workshop, consisted of a traveling flatbed truck that would perform free Shakespeare in the Lower East Side and other neighborhoods. While the decision to open that theater (which was called the Public) with a rock-and-roll musical about hippies took many people by surprise, the two other theater groups central to its creation, the Open Theater and the La MaMa Experimental Theater Club, were more logical incubators.

The Open Theater was formally created in 1963 by a group of Nola Chilton's students when the noted acting teacher emigrated to Israel. Among its members were Joseph Chaikin, who became the artistic director of the group, and Gerome Ragni, who gave the Open Theater its name. Ragni's experimental work was admired by the likes of the British director Peter Brook, who made a huge splash on Broadway in 1965 with *Marat/Sade*. However, more mainstream directors were also fond of the effervescent young man known to all as "Jerry": John Gielgud cast Ragni in a small role in his 1964 production of *Hamlet* starring Richard Burton.

Immediately after that production, Ragni performed off-Broadway in *Hang Down Your Head and Die*, a capital-punishment-themed revue, where he met a promising musician named James Rado. Ragni, a Pittsburgh native from a big Italian family, and Rado, whose family had bounced from California to New York to Washington, D.C., were both born in the mid-1930s and had both served in the military before moving to New York.

Nonetheless, the two had traveled in fairly different theatrical circles. While Ragni gravitated toward the downtown experimental theater scene, Rado—who had studied with the legendary acting coach Lee Strasberg—struggled to make a name for himself as a songwriter before landing a series of Broadway roles, including the Actors' Studio production of *Marathon '33* and *The Lion in Winter*, in which he played Richard the Lionheart. Rado and Ragni quickly bonded, and while *Hang Down Your Head* closed on opening night, they were soon cast in the hit comedy *The Knack*.

It was around this time, in early 1965, that they became fascinated by the youth culture of Greenwich Village and began to amass material for a musical about the

ABOVE AND TOP Fashion and society were also undergoing seismic changes at the time of *HAIR*'s creation, which fed into the show.

passionate, idealistic iconoclasts who would soon be known as hippies. They also frequented museums and galleries together, and one of these trips would give their project its name. "We didn't have a title at first," Rado says. "About a month earlier, we had seen a painting at the Whitney Museum called *Hair* [by Jim Dine.] I called Jerry's attention to it and said, 'Hey, that's an odd name for a painting.' And then one day Jerry said we should call the play *HAIR*."

Another admirer of Ragni and later Rado was Ellen Stewart, who had opened the La MaMa Experimental Theater Club in 1961. Stewart offered the Open Theater a season-long residency in the mid-1960s, and it was there that Ragni would appear in Megan Terry's *Viet Rock*. While this vehemently antiwar play was not a musical per se, it did include six songs performed on acoustic guitar, and the company's exploratory development process would prove extremely influential in Ragni's next Vietnam-related musical project, *HAIR*, which also had its genesis in an Open Theater workshop. *Viet Rock* would also provide Ragni with the pretext to approach Joseph Papp, the impresario of the Public.

In addition to hosting the Open Theater, La MaMa had its own acting troupe run by Tom O'Horgan, one of the more innovative directors in an increasingly vibrant downtown scene. O'Horgan, a Chicago native who played dozens of musical instruments, had imported from that city the "theater games" made famous by Viola Spolin and her son, Paul Sills. These exercises were designed to foster trust and interdependence among the members of an acting company, blurring or even eliminating the boundaries between the actors and their roles.

The La MaMa Troupe, as it was called, scored a critical success using these methods in 1967 with the absurdist play *Futz!*, about a farmer who falls in love with his pig. Among those who saw it were Rado and Ragni, who introduced themselves to O'Horgan after the show and asked him to direct the premiere of their own theater piece. O'Horgan, who was directing a European tour of *Futz!* when the Public Theater production took place, was unable to accept at the time, and the authors reportedly also considered Chaikin before Gerald Freedman, the artistic director of the Public, agreed to direct *HAIR*.

A lesser-known factor in the creation of *HAIR* was the short-lived American Theatre Laboratory, which director/choreographer Jerome Robbins had founded in 1966. Ragni had shifted his allegiances to this group that same year after a schism within the Open Theater, and Robbins met with Rado and Ragni several times about their fledgling project. "Robbins gave us wonderful advice and came up with very constructive criticism," Ragni told Barbara Lee Horn, the author of *The Age of HAIR*. Anna Sokolow and Julie Arenal—the choreographers of the off-Broadway and Broadway *HAIR* mountings, respectively—would also come from Robbins's group, and Freedman had assisted Robbins on Broadway shows like *West Side Story* and *Gypsy*.

Today, the Public routinely transfers its projects to Broadway (recent transfers include *Passing Strange, Topdog/Underdog*, and, of course, the 2009 *HAIR* revival,) while La MaMa has built a formidable reputation as a home for envelope-pushing theater troupes and authors from around the world. At the time, though, the prospect of a play bursting from the East Village to global fame was ludicrous. A train ride from New Haven to New York would begin to change that.

ABOVE The Gaslight Café on MacDougal Street was a coffee house that became a vibrant part of the West Village cultural scene in New York.

LEFT Ellen Stewart, seen here in 2000, has supported off-off-Broadway for nearly 50 years through her La MaMa Experimental Theater Club.

FAR LEFT A group of street musicians play in Washington Square Park, which became a central gathering place for New York's hippie population.

PREAMBLE TO THE PUBLIC

Shortly upon being appointed dean of the Yale School of Drama in 1966, the esteemed theater critic Robert Brustein invited several notables from New York's experimental theater scene to New Haven, Connecticut for professorships and residencies. One such person was Joseph Papp, the pugnacious impresario who had brought Shakespeare to the masses, staring down powerful establishment figures like the formidable urban planner Robert Moses in the process.

The invitation came at a pivotal time for Papp. It was the fall of 1966, and he was in the middle of an ambitious campaign to convert the abandoned Astor Library on Manhattan's Lafayette Street into a multi-theater complex known as the Public Theater. Papp's reputation had been built on accessible, rough-and-tumble productions of Shakespeare, and his organization was called the New York Shakespeare Festival. He was also excited about the prospect of working with new playwrights at the Public.

Another Brustein invitee was the Open Theater, which presented its acclaimed production of *Viet Rock* at Yale. One night that October in 1966, exactly one year before *HAIR* opened at the Public Theater, on the train ride back to New York, Gerome Ragni, an actor in *Viet Rock*, approached Papp, for whom he had auditioned several times, to show him the first script of a new piece that he and James Rado were writing.

"He showed me a dog-eared piece of paper with some notes on it," Papp told Cue magazine in 1970. "The material sounded interesting. I followed it through and before I knew it, I said, 'Let's open the theater with this work.' It was *HAIR*." As is often the case with a showman of Papp's nature, several statements in this fairly brief quote need to be contextualized or outright corrected. For one thing, Ragni actually gave Papp a fully bound script (one that Rado has to this day.) In the meantime, the two authors had passed a copy of their script through Isabelle Blau, who had befriended Ragni at the Open Theater, to her ex-husband Eric Blau. After reading it, he talked to Rado on the phone with great interest in the project and found out that the authors were looking for a composer to set their lyrics to music. Blau, who would soon find his attention consumed by his own hit 1968 musical, *Jacques Brel Is Alive and Living in Paris*, which he cowrote, approached his acquaintance Nat Shapiro, a well-connected Columbia Records executive, for help in finding a suitable composer. Shapiro brought a first draft of the script home and asked his 15-yearr-old daughter, Amy, for her input. Amy Louise Pommier, as she is now known, has distinct memories of reading it on the floor of their family friend Michel Legrand's living room while listening to the brand-new Beatles album *Sgt. Pepper's Lonely Hearts Club Band* on headsets. This makes her the first person remotely close in age to the show's characters to have experienced it. (She says she liked it quite a bit.)

ABOVE Papp sits on the steps of the Delacorte Theater in Central Park, which opened in 1962.

ABOVE Anna Sokolow, seen here in 1958, served first as choreographer and then as director of the Public Theater production of *HAIR*.

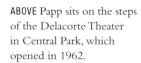

RIGHT Sasha Allen leads the cast in "Aquarius" during the 2009 Broadway revival.

AQUARIUS

When the moon is in the Seventh House
And Jupiter aligns with Mars
Then peace will guide the planets
And love will steer the stars

This is the dawning of the age of Aquarius
The age of Aquarius
Aquarius!
Aquarius!

Harmony and understanding
Sympathy and trust abounding
No more falsehood or derision
Golden living dreams of visions
Mystic crystal revelation
And the mind's true liberation
Aquarius!
Aquarius!

When the moon is in the Seventh House
And Jupiter aligns with Mars
Then peace will guide the planets
And love will steer the stars

This is the dawning of the age of Aquarius
The age of Aquarius
Aquarius!
Aquarius!

"Aquarius"

In lieu of an overture, this song introduced the concept of an age to which the tribe aspired, one that would bring "the mind's true liberation." Gerald Freedman had originally positioned it at the end of Claude's acid trip as a sort of musical rebirth. Incidentally, some astrologers object to the first line of the song: The moon is in the seventh house on a daily basis, and Jupiter aligns with Mars several times a year.

JAMES RADO: *"When one age gives way to another, there's a period where they overlap, which is called the cusp or the dawning. It lasts about 200 years, so the song still works for a while."*

GALT MACDERMOT: *"That's the one song in the whole show that I rewrote. The lyrics were so spacy that I tried to write a spacy tune. They didn't like it, and I didn't either, so I rewrote it."*

JAMES RADO: *"Gerry didn't think the first melody was effective, I suppose."*

GERALD FREEDMAN: *"I still think using 'Aquarius' as a resurrection number is better than blowing your stack on the first number."*

AIN'T GOT NO

I'm black I'm black
I'm pink I'm pink
I'm Rinso white
I'm in-vis-i-ble

[WOOF]
Ain't got no home
[TRIBE]
So
[WOOF]
Ain't got no shoes
[TRIBE]
Poor
[WOOF]
Ain't got no money
[TRIBE]
Honey
[WOOF]
Ain't got no class
[TRIBE]
Common
[WOOF]
Ain't got no scarf
[TRIBE]
Hot
[WOOF]
Ain't got no gloves
[TRIBE]
Cold
[WOOF]
Ain't got no bed
[TRIBE]
Beat
[WOOF]
Ain't got no pot
[TRIBE]
Busted
[WOOF]
Ain't got no faith
[TRIBE]
Catholic

[HUD]
Ain't got no mother
[TRIBE]
Orphan
[HUD]
Ain't got no culture
[TRIBE]
Man
[HUD]
Ain't got no friends
[TRIBE]
Lucky
[HUD]
Ain't got no schoolin'
[TRIBE]
Dumb
[HUD]
Ain't got no shine
[TRIBE]
Dull
[HUD]
Ain't got no underwear
[TRIBE]
Bad
[HUD]
Ain't got no soap
[TRIBE]
Dirty
[HUD]
Ain't got no A-Train
[TRIBE]
Jump
[HUD]
Ain't got no mind
[TRIBE]
Lost it

[DIONNE]
Ain't got no smokes
[TRIBE]
Shit
[DIONNE]
Ain't got no job
[TRIBE]
Lazy
[DIONNE]
Ain't got no work
[TRIBE]
Fine
[DIONNE]
Ain't got no coins
[TRIBE]
Broke
[DIONNE]
Ain't got no pennies
[TRIBE]
Beg
[DIONNE]
Ain't got no girl/man
[TRIBE]
Horny
[DIONNE]
Ain't got no ticket
[TRIBE]
Hustle
[DIONNE]
Ain't got no token
[TRIBE]
Walk
[DIONNE]
Ain't got no God
[TRIBE]
Good

"Ain't Got No"

As individual members of the tribe list everything they lack, from gloves and underwear to class and faith, the rest of the tribe respond with terse and often hostile descriptions: dumb, dirty, common. It is preceded by a brief number called "I'm Black," which includes a bit of foreshadowing in which Claude sings, "I'm invisible."

JAMES RADO: *"The echoes become a little cheeky here, I guess."*

GALT MACDERMOT: *"This goes over much better now than before."*

JAMES RADO: *"There were two songs that were written before Jerry and I ever met. Jerry came in with 'Ain't Got No,' and I had 'Where Do I Go?' 'Ain't Got No' was in his notebook, and I remember it was one of the things that really impressed me about him."*

ABOVE From top, Leata
Galloway, James Rado, and
Steve Curry, rehearse.

Shapiro met the authors and recommended Herbie Hancock as a possible collaborator. The lyric of the title song "HAIR" was sent to Hancock and came back professionally notated on music paper, but he had chosen to set only some of the words, in a new order, to music. This was not what Rado and Ragni had in mind. The undaunted Shapiro had just met a composer who had recently emigrated to New York from Montreal. In an article for *ASCAP Today* magazine, Shapiro described how he thought of Galt MacDermot, a Canadian-born composer who had gone to college in South Africa and whose instrumental "African Waltz" had won a Grammy Award in 1960. Shapiro thought MacDermot, with whom he would often discuss jazz, might make a good collaborator despite being completely different from Rado and Ragni. "Galt, who has four children, a square haircut, and (how far out can you get?) lives in Staten Island, was just wildly and weirdly creative enough to do the job," Shapiro wrote. He went on to call MacDermot "one of the few mature, technically equipped musicians around who is not only aware of what is happening in popular music but understands and loves the roots and the dynamics of the new thing."

MacDermot met with Rado first. "We got along," he recalls. After what Shapiro described as "a somewhat tenuous exploratory meeting with the authors in a booth at Howard Johnson's," MacDermot headed back to Staten island and quickly went to work, writing music for "Aquarius" and several other songs within 36 hours.

In the meantime, Rado and Ragni received a phone call from Papp at the Public Theater saying he was excited by the script and was considering it for production. They told him that they had just found their composer and the music was beginning to take shape. He invited them to his office at the Public Theater so he could hear it. The three of them arrived at the newly demolished interior of the Astor Library on Lafayette Street just below Astor Place in the East Village. His office was huge and contained Papp's very large desk and an upright piano. Rado and Ragni didn't know the music well enough yet to sing it so they sat back and listened while MacDermot played the piano and sang the songs for him. While Galt's voice was very quiet, his phrasing was impeccable and Papp was immediately taken by the music's rhythms and melodies. Rado remembered telling Papp during the meeting that Tom O'Horgan was their favorite director. Rado and Ragni had admired his work on *Futz!* Rado says, "His style seemed very of the moment in conjuring the hippie atmosphere." Unfortunately, O'Horgan was booked to leave on a tour of Europe with his LaMama troupe and was not available. Papp suggested Gerald Freedman instead and asked them to wait outside his office. Rado recalls, "We waited a good half hour before we were called back in and told that the Public Theater's first production would be *HAIR*."

"Joe asked me to read the material," Freedman says remembering his first exposure to the script he received from Papp, "and what was impressive about it was the energy. But when you see a piece of paper that just says, 'Hair Hair Hair Hair Hair' it was both puzzling and exciting." Ming Cho Lee, who designed the set at the Public, would express similar bafflement at the same piece.

Soon after Papp set up a meeting with Freedman. MacDermot, Rado, and Ragni went to Freedman's apartment on West 87th Street. Because Rado and Ragni had still not learned the songs, MacDermot played and sang the score for Freedman and dance arranger John Morris who would later become the show's musical director. The three couldn't tell what Freedman's reaction was at the time. MacDermot had the feeling that Freedman didn't respond favorably to what he heard. "He didn't like the songs and didn't want to do it." MacDermot says now.

The authors, who were interested in seeing *HAIR* reach as broad an audience as possible, now auditioned their material for Broadway producers. The mere suggestion of a musical about hippies was enough to dissuade David Merrick. Harold Prince and Robert Whitehead were similarly unswayed. Soon after the authors received another call from the Public Theater saying Papp had changed his mind. Rado heard Papp say, "We've decided to open instead with a new British play called *Sargeant Musgrave's Dance*." They were devastated by the news.

At this point Rado and Ragni learned the songs and sang them at several new auditions their agent had arranged. As they performed them over and over again they realized how powerful these songs were and decided to call Papp again to convince him to give them another chance. Papp, persuaded, invited them back and this time was joined in his office by Bernard Gersten and Gerald Freedman. Rado and Ragni sang the songs with much more gusto this time and Papp loved how MacDermot had set the words to music. The authors were again asked to wait outside for over 45 minutes this time before they were ushered back inside and told that they had changed their minds and the Public Theater would open with *HAIR* as originally promised. Gerald Freedman would direct the show and he, in turn, selected the modern dance choreographer Anna Sokolow, a veteran of Martha Graham's company as well as of Jerome Robbin's American Theatre Laboratory—and, like Freedman, a professor at Julliard—to choreograph. The pieces were in place for what would be, even by the often chaotic standards of downtown theater, a turbulent production.

TOP The cast rehearses for the off-Broadway production, probably a scene in which they mime riding on the New York subway.

ABOVE Jonelle Allen played Dionne at the Public but did not continue to Broadway when the production transferred.

RIGHT The original Broadway cast performs the title song.

HAIR

She asks me why
I'm just a hairy guy
I'm hairy noon and night
Hair that's a fright
I'm hairy high and low
Don't ask me why
Don't know
It's not for lack of bread
Like the Grateful Dead
Darling

Gimme a head with hair
Long beautiful hair
Shining, gleaming,
Steaming, flaxen, waxen

Give me down to there hair
Shoulder length or longer
Here baby, there mama
Everywhere daddy daddy

Hair, hair, hair, hair, hair, hair, hair
Flow it, show it
Long as God can grow it
My hair

Let it fly in the breeze
And get caught in the trees
Give a home to the fleas in my hair
A home for fleas
A hive for bees
A nest for birds
There ain't no words
For the beauty, the splendor, the wonder
Of my...

Hair, hair, hair, hair, hair, hair, hair
Flow it, show it
Long as God can grow it
My hair

I want it long, straight, curly, fuzzy
Snaggy, shaggy, ratty, matty
Oily, greasy, fleecy
Shining, gleaming, steaming
Flaxen, waxen
Knotted, polka-dotted
Twisted, beaded, braided
Powdered, flowered, and confettied
Bangled, tangled, spangled, and
spaghettied!

Oh say can you see
My eyes if you can
Then my hair's too short

Down to here
Down to there
I want hair
It stops by itself

They'll be ga ga at the go go
When they see me in my toga
My toga made of blond
Brilliantined
Biblical hair

My hair like Jesus wore it
Hallelujah I adore it
Hallelujah Mary loved her son
Why don't my mother love me?

Hair, hair, hair, hair, hair, hair, hair
Flow it, show it
Long as God can grow it
My hair, hair, hair, hair, hair, hair, hair
Flow it, show it
Long as God can grow it
My hair

"Hair"

Claude, Berger, and the tribe extol the virtues of "shining, gleaming, steaming, flaxen, waxen" hair, "long as God can grow it."

GALT MACDERMOT: *"This is a song that, for some reason, works very well. I never thought of it as a showstopper. Jim was very proud of it, but they made him rewrite it. That was redone—and to its advantage."*

JAMES RADO: *"It's an ecstatic song, the same way 'I Got Life' is. These are songs of excitement."*

PUBLIC THEATER

The din of the Public Theater offices, already significant with construction work under way, grew considerably as *HAIR* began to fall into place. Bernard Gersten, who met Papp back in the 1940s and went on to spend 18 years as associate producer of the Public, distinctly recalls his first exposure to the score. His and Papp's offices were separated by an interior office that housed each of their assistants. "My first memory of the show is coming in one day and hearing the sound of Galt's feet pounding as he played *HAIR* in Joe's office. The sound went clear through to my office." (It was at Gersten's desk that Rado later fiddled around with embellishments to the standard "A New Musical" subtitle, finally coming up with "The American Tribal Love-Rock Musical" after about two hours. "'Love-rock' was Galt's music," he says.)

Auditions began in the summer of 1967, and an early sticking point was the casting of the two lead roles, Claude and Berger. Rado and Ragni had based the parts on themselves, but Freedman feared that they were too old to play teenagers. He gradually came around to the idea of Ragni as Berger: "I could never find anyone who had the manic energy of Jerry—it was totally unique. Berger is *sui generis,* and so I thought age was irrelevant there." He drew the line, however, at Rado, and hired an actor named Walker Daniels to play Claude. Among the other performers cast were Shelley Plimpton, a waifish cashier at a coffee house that Rado and Ragni wandered into one night; Sally Eaton, who was spotted playing guitar as well as modeling during a fashion show on Second Avenue; and Linda Compton, Paul Jabara, and Suzannah Evans, a group of former high-school classmates from Bay Ridge, Brooklyn, who dreamed of becoming a folk-rock trio.

An additional hurdle came when Anna Sokolow was hospitalized with appendicitis immediately before rehearsals began. It was decided that Sokolow would miss the first 10 days and then choreograph the show upon her return. In the meantime, Freedman—whose time working under Jerome Robbins gave him a certain degree of comfort with dance—would set up what amounted to placeholder dances, "to get them on their feet because it had to be done."

Tensions between Freedman and his two librettists/lyricists, began mounting within hours of the first rehearsal. Rado and Ragni viewed their director as a relic from a more straitlaced era, while Freedman bristled at their constant rewriting of the script. "You never knew when someone nailed something or whether they nailed something for the afternoon and it wouldn't be repeatable," he said of Rado and Ragni's methods. He also felt that too many of the songs were inessential to the narrative: Several of the earlier numbers were cut, and it was only after repeated pleas from MacDermot that "Frank Mills" stayed in the show.

The hope was that Sokolow's arrival would defuse tensions, but it had the opposite effect. Rado and Ragni began playing Freedman and Sokolow against each other, and before long the two were not on speaking terms. "A lot goes

ABOVE (left to right) James Rado, Gerome Ragni, and Galt MacDermot.

RIGHT Warren Burton, a tribe member in the 1967 production of *HAIR*.

THE TRIBE CLAUDE HOOPER BUKOWSKI

Born in "dirty, slummy, mucky, polluted Flushing"—not Manchester, England, as he would have you believe. The only member we see interacting with his family. Dreams of being a movie director, something he voiced more strongly in the Public/Cheetah version. Grapples publicly and frequently with his obligations to his country, his friends, and himself. Loves Sheila and, less overtly, Berger.

Many a doctoral dissertation has been made comparing Claude to Jesus, to Hamlet, to the Apollonian half of a unified whole completed by the Dionysian Berger. Textual support can be found for each of these comparisons, but Claude is first and foremost a confused kid with an unlucky draft number and a crush (or two.)

Most of the millions of people who attended *HAIR* were not hippies. They had not burned their draft cards or been kicked out of school or dropped acid. But they did have a degree of ambivalence about Vietnam, about America, about their future. Claude Bukowski—the last name was Rado's mother's maiden name—was an entry point for those men and women who wanted to understand the hippies as well as gawk at them.

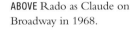

ABOVE Rado as Claude on Broadway in 1968.

RIGHT Sally Eaton, the original Jeanie.

BELOW Steve Dean, the original Woof, and Ragni rehearse at the Public.

on in the first 10 days of a show, and she wasn't part of that life," says Amy Saltz, Freedman's assistant. "I think that must have been very difficult for her, and she was still in a lot of pain." Eaton, who played Jeanie, is less charitable: "Anna made changes without informing Mr. Freedman, contradicted him in front of the cast, and openly disparaged his work." Rado and Ragni, meanwhile, sent Papp so many multipage "memos" about their conception of the show and how it was being violated that one such epistle came back to them torn into pieces.

It finally proved to be too much for Freedman, who went to Papp during the last week of rehearsal and offered to step down from the production. ("I was somewhat chastened and disappointed when Joe accepted," he says.) Sokolow and Rado took over as co-directors, and Rado also replaced Walker Daniels as Claude.

"The cast was totally confused," says Saltz, who had been willing to step down with Freedman but stayed on, nominally as Sokolow's assistant. "I basically watched Anna do what Anna was doing and tried to calm the cast down," she says of her new responsibilities. Sokolow's brusque demeanor quickly alienated many of the actors. "There was some physical thing she had two people do," Saltz says, "and they said they had a bunch of lines 10 seconds later. And she said, 'I don't care about that! Do what I tell you to! Don't question me!' And some of the people who did question her were fired." Meanwhile, the rewrites kept coming.

The decision to open the Public with *HAIR* has become deeply intertwined with the iconic status of both the show and the theater. Papp, who had already sliced in half his initial ambition of presenting eight shows in two theaters during the first Public season, hoped to open his theater in the fall of 1967 with *Stock Up on Pepper Cause Turkey's Going to War*, a bleak split-personality comedy by a homeless alcoholic named Frank Zajac. However, construction on the Anspacher

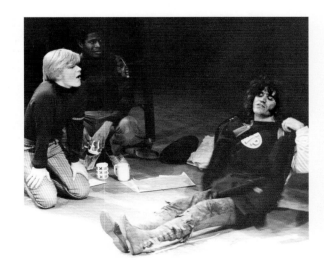

MANCHESTER ENGLAND

Manchester England England
Across the Atlantic Sea
And I'm a genius genius
I believe in God
And I believe that God
Believes in Claude
That's me that's me

Claude Hooper Bukowski
Finds that it's groovy
To hide in a movie
Pretends he's Fellini
And Antonioni
And also his countryman Roman
Polanski
All rolled into one
One Claude Hooper Bukowski

Now that I've dropped out
Why is life dreary dreary?
Answer my weary query
Timothy Leary dearie

Manchester England England
Across the Atlantic Sea
And I'm a genius genius
I believe in God
And I believe that God
Believes in Claude
That's me (that's he)
That's me (that's he)
That's me (that's he)
That's me

"Manchester England"

Claude's Anglophilia shines through this uptempo slice of early-'60s-style pop.

JAMES RADO: *"We did that because of Albert Finney in* Saturday Night, Sunday Morning. *That was one of the first of a spate of movies set in the North Country of England. We saw that movie and loved it, even though we couldn't understand half the dialogue."*

GALT MACDERMOT: *"I used a shuffle, which was just going out of style at that time."*

PUBLIC THEATER

I GOT LIFE

I got life, mother
I got laughs, sister
I got freedom, brother
I got good times, man

I got crazy ways, daughter
I got million-dollar charm, cousin
I got headaches and toothaches
And bad times too
Like you

I got my hair
I got my head
I got my brains
I got my ears
I got my eyes
I got my nose
I got my mouth
I got my teeth
I got my tongue
I got my chin
I got my neck
I got my tits
I got my heart
I got my soul
I got my back
I got my ass
I got my arms
I got my hands
I got my fingers
Got my legs
I got my feet
I got my toes
I got my liver
Got my blood

I got my guts (I got my guts)
I got my muscles (muscles)
I got life (life)
Life (life)
Life (life)
LIFE!

"I Got Life"

When Claude's mother asks him what he's got that makes him "so damn superior," he responds with this propulsive hymn to every inch of himself.

JAMES RADO: *"Claude is a very positive, up, crazy, fully alive person, and I think that comes through best here."*

GALT MACDERMOT: *"Jim used to stop the show with it, and Gavin [Creel] comes close now. If the lyric is repetitious, like this one is, you just need to find the right tune and let it flow."*

Theater, the first of what would ultimately be five performance spaces in the Public, went over schedule, and Papp asked his friend Ellen Stewart if he could direct *Stock Up…* at La MaMa instead. When the Anspacher was finally ready, *HAIR* inherited the honor of christening the theater.

Papp was slated to direct the Public's second show, a radical deconstruction of *Hamlet* starring Martin Sheen that would open in the Anspacher just nine days after the first show's scheduled closing. (This tight turnaround would have an enormous impact on the future of *HAIR*.) Perhaps because of the preparation involved in directing *Hamlet*, Papp was truly surprised by what he saw when he sat in on *HAIR*'s final dress rehearsal—and not in a good way. He immediately fired Sokolow and sent a telegram to Freedman, who had headed to Washington, D.C.: "PLEASE COME BACK."

Freedman agreed to resume control of the show on two conditions. For one thing, the staging would revert to where it had been when he left, including much of the stopgap choreography he had created before Sokolow joined rehearsals. The other condition was that Rado once again vacate the role of Claude. Papp agreed to both terms, and the cast and crew went to work putting *HAIR* back together again. It was October 15, two days before the first preview performance. "On Tuesday, we restored the first act," Freedman says. "There was a performance that night, and we did—for lack of a better phrase—my first act and Anna's second act. On Wednesday, we restored the second act." He and Sokolow went to arbitration not long after, and it was ruled that the *HAIR* on display at the Public was solely Freedman's creation; however, many parties involved—most notably Julie Arenal, who would choreograph the Broadway version—maintain that Sokolow's aesthetic remained clearly visible.

The eight-week Public run of *HAIR* was as a distant cousin to the show that would sprout to life on Broadway less than six months later. Freedman's experience in the traditional theater yielded a combination of earnestness and verve with the

LEFT The Stockholm, Sweden, cast performs "I Got Life" in 1968.

ABOVE Suzannah Evans and Paul Jabara rehearse at the Public.

BELOW Warren Burton as an American Indian during the trip sequence in Act II.

drollery and outright silliness that was such a crucial part of Rado and Ragni's arsenal. Below is a synopsis of what these first audiences saw:

After an Apparition briefly appears and two adult figures sing "Red, Blue and White," Claude Bukowski delivers a self-explanatory monologue. ("I'm a genius; I believe in God. I believe in meself, too, but I don't know how long me old man's gonna put up with that, do I?") He is joined first by Berger and then by Woof and Hud; after divulging that he and Hud are ex-cons, Woof sings "Ain't Got No." A school principal expels Berger—"one of your rebellious beatnik leaders"—and says, "Maybe it's time Society cried HELP!" Berger describes himself as "anti-everything" before joining Claude in a reprise of "Ain't Got No." Claude sings a snippet of "Manchester England;" wards off his mother, who has stripped down to a slip; and then sings "I Got Life." The tribe reprises "Ain't Got No" on the way to a rally, then Jeanie appears and sings "Air."

The action then moves to the Intergalactic Bathtub club, where the tribe sings "Initials" and Berger announces his expulsion with "Going Down." Much of the cast affects a British accent *à la* Claude. Claude unveils the news that he has been drafted and reads a poem called "Ode to a Stick." Woof counsels him about how to beat the draft board by acting like a homosexual in a song called "Nervous Nellie." Claude then sings "Hair" to a curious couple, complete with this verse:

> My barber's name is Delilah
> Don't touch me Delilah
> Here's your two-fifty plus a tip
> I think your service is a gyp
> But I'll pay it yes I'll pay
> Just so you'll stay away

The anthropological theory that would become "My Conviction" is presented here as spoken text. ("Colored Spade" was treated similarly upon Hud's first entrance.) The ensuing stretch of music-free material—much of it about the love triangle between Claude, Berger, and Sheila—is long by the standards of any musical, let alone one as melody-stuffed as *HAIR*.

It includes this graphic stage direction: "BERGER has just fucked SHEILA in public. Or rather RAPED her in public. BERGER has had his orgasm. SHE was fighting him off and reacts to his attack." She and Claude then have a lengthy scene together in which he describes a movie script that he has written for her and the rest of the tribe. Claude briefly quotes *Hamlet* ("O that this too too solid flesh would melt") and talks about being a patriot despite his ambivalence to the war. The love triangle becomes a rectangle as Jeanie's love for Claude becomes clear.

Sheila then sings "Dead End," followed by, in rapid succession, the Apparition returning to sing "Mess o' Dirt," Crissy singing "Frank Mills," and the "Be-In." This last song features characters referred to as "Puppet Cops" as well as the two adult authority figures, who sing these angry lyrics: "Bad diction / Have pimples / Dress funny / No money / Chew finger nails / Play in the mud / Riot riot riot riot riot riot riot riot."

Claude sings "Where Do I Go?" at the Be-In, ultimately joined by the rest of the tribe. But not before an announcer makes the following—and, some have argued, prophetic—statement: "Tourists. See the Hippies … See the freak show.

See THEM … the Gypsy Tribes … Watch safely through our shatterproof sky dome bus-o-rama. See, see, see the Hippie Phenomenon."

Act II begins with "Electric Blues," and then a trio sings "Easy to Be Hard," as Berger tries to coerce Sheila to have sex with Claude before he goes off to war. A clean-cut Claude appears, which spurs three of the black women to sing "White Boys;" a trio of white women follows suit with "Black Boys." "Walking in Space" kicks off a mass trip that includes paratroopers, Indians, black militants (including the playwright and poet LeRoi Jones,) a spoken version of "Yes, I's Finished on Y'All's Farmlands…," "Abie Baby" (but not the accompanying riff on the Emancipation Proclamation,) mass death, and a 1,000-Year-Old Man who sings "So Sing the Children on the Avenue."

After Claude mimes his death, the entire cast is resurrected to the tune of "Aquarius." Claude and Berger speak the "What a piece of work is man" monologue from *Hamlet*, and this segues into "Good Morning Starshine." The action shifts to the apartment that Sheila shares with a gay roommate. Claude confides to her that he actually comes from the idyllic planet "Exanaplanetooch":

> The buildings in the cities
> Shaped like hills
> Made of black and green
> And blue and yellow glass
> With rivers running through them
> Crystal bright

This tactic, coupled with his imminent departure, succeeds in seducing Sheila, who sings "The Climax." The next morning, a newly shorn Claude rejoins the tribe and presents his hair to Berger in a brown paper bag. A handful of female cast members wind up an array of miniature tanks, guns, and other war toys all over the stage as the two adults express their pride in Claude for heading off to Vietnam. "THEY exit and the lights dim slowly as the war instruments sputter, flash, wheel about and explode flames and the GIRLS silently walk around the stage area. Note: Possible singing of 'SENTIMENTAL ENDING' or 'AQUARIUS.'" ("Sentimental Ending"—the lyric consists entirely of the title phrase spoken again and again at an increasingly fast speed to replicate the accelerating train that whisked Claude away—was a light-hearted poke at the standard musical-theater conventions that *HAIR* would do so much to dismantle.)

The Claude/Sheila/Berger love triangle is a perfectly serviceable device on which to hang a plot, and in a decade that began with *Jules and Jim* and ended with *Butch Cassidy and the Sundance Kid*, having a pretty girl on one arm and an even prettier boy on the other, albeit somewhat ambiguously in the latter case, had become a key sign of countercultural bona fides. But the sketchy depictions of the trio's friends, of their tribesmen and women, prevent the communal nature of this ad hoc group from fully being established.

At the same time, the fate of Claude, while less explicit than in later versions of *HAIR*, arguably resonates more deeply in the 1967 telling. The scene with his mother and the since-discarded "Delilah" stanza to the title song add some intriguing shadings to his sexual confusion, and any disruption in momentum from "Exanaplanetooch" is offset by a poetic streak that differentiates Claude more forcefully from Berger.

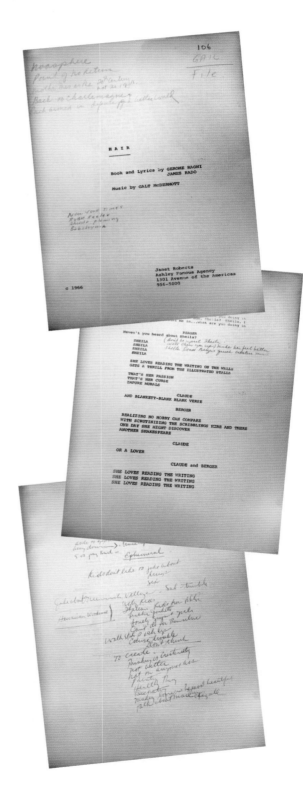

BELOW This original script from the Public features handwritten notes from both Rado (in pencil) and Ragni (in red pen.)   RIGHT Ragni in action.

"Dead End"

The list of proscriptions continues, this time through a series of street signs (reflected in the stencils on the floor of Robin Wagner's 1968 set.) The song came and went from the Broadway production, sung at different times by Sheila and a group of tribe members.

GALT MACDERMOT: *"It was more or less an introductory song, but it was too long to be an introductory song."*

JAMES RADO: *"'Dead End' isn't in this [2009] production. I'd love to have it in there right after 'I Got Life' and tear the house down twice in a row. It started out as a Sheila song, with Jill O'Hara singing it off-Broadway. We would've taken her to Broadway, but she took* Promises, Promises *instead. I loved her voice."*

AMY SALTZ: *"I remember walking into the green room on my first day of rehearsals, and Galt was teaching 'Dead End' to Jill O'Hara. My jaw just dropped."*

NATALIE MOSCO (ORIGINAL BROADWAY CAST MEMBER): *"'Dead End' was out until Galt had enough power to get the black people in the tribe to sing that song."*

DEAD END

Dead end
Don't walk
Keep out
Red light

Steep cliff
Beware
Mad dog
Blind man

Warning land mine
High voltage line
Don't make a pass
Keep off the grass

Detour
Wet paint
Hands off
Dead end

Sharp curve
Steep hill
Danger
One-way

Emergency
Exit
Only
Only

Warning markers hidden
Loitering forbitten
All trespassers will be shot
Claude loves Sheila—he better love her not

Wet paint
Hands off
Keep out
Dead end

Men working
Dead end
No standing
Dead end

No parking
Dead end
No smoking
Dead end

No joking
Dead end
My friend

YES, I'S FINISHED ON Y'ALL'S FARMLANDS

Yes, I's finished on y'all's farm land With yo' boll weevils and all,
and pluckin' y'all's chickens, fryin' mother's oats in grease.
I's free now, thanks to yo', Massa Lincoln, emancipator of the slaves.

Yes, I's finished on y'all's farm land with yo' boll weevils and all,
and pluckin' y'all's chickens, fryin' mother's oats in grease.
I's free now, thanks to yo', Massa Lincoln, emancipator of the slaves.
Yeah, yeah, yeah, emanci-motherfuckin-pator of the slaves.
Yeah, yeah, yeah, emanci-motherfuckin-pator of the slaves.

"Yes, I's Finished on Y'All's Farmlands"

A quartet of black actors sing in Negro dialect their tribute to Abe Lincoln, "emanci-motherfuckin'-pator of the slaves."

JAMES RADO: *"It's a little bit Stepin Fetchit. We liked the humor that provoked."*

GALT MACDERMOT: *"To me, that's funny. That's using the language of the South to make fun of it."*

TOP A tribe member dresses as an Indian during his Act II acid trip.

RIGHT Susan Batson played a fellow Indian in the same scene.

OPPOSITE ABOVE Gerome Ragni as Berger.

THE TRIBE GEORGE BERGER

Hates being called George. "Dematriculates" from high school for violating the dress code. First seen searching for a 16-year-old virgin named Donna. Loves everyone, including Berger.

Berger is the show's most flamboyant character, equal parts ringmaster, trickster, liberator, and loose cannon. *The New York Times* theater critic Clive Barnes described Berger as a "psychedelic teddy bear" when he reviewed *HAIR* at the Public, and the description was so apt that the authors added this line to Berger's first monologue.

The only truly objectionable behavior in the show from the hippies' perspective comes from Berger: when he tears up the shirt that Sheila gives him, and more crucially in the scene (cut for Broadway) where Berger is described as having raped Sheila. In both versions, Berger tries to persuade Sheila to sleep with Claude as a sort of going-away present, but his exhortations are much stronger in the earlier version.

These developments, and the many that came after them as *HAIR* continued its accelerated path to infamy, are only as effective as the form that holds them. On a structural level, it is reasonable to wonder whether Rado and Ragni, constantly throwing over their previous ideas in favor of the rantings of a bedraggled restaurant patron or a chunk of Shakespeare or a letter to the editor in the *Village Voice* (all of which would ultimately make their way into the show as songs,) would have ever completed anything without a Gerald Freedman to mold these notions into a coherent whole. "I don't think it would have had a life if it hadn't been given a structure," Freedman says of his contribution to this admittedly rough first draft of the show. "Giving it a form allowed it to be seen." Bernard Gersten, who was overseeing much of the show's progress—or lack thereof—while Papp was preparing *Hamlet*, is even more direct in his estimation of Freedman's contributions: "Gerry took what was very raw material and gave it shape and fought for the narrative of the play. He was the catalytic agent for *HAIR*."

However it had reached this point, *HAIR* was ready to be seen after years of brainstorming and weeks of rancor. Among the first paying customers was the man who would turn the show into his life's work, a polo-playing politician from Oak Brook, Illinois, who came to the Public expecting to see a show about Indians and left with something close to a mission.

ABOVE A questionnaire that Joseph Papp distributed to *HAIR* audiences at the Public.

EARLY STEPS

"*HAIR*" quickly sold out at the Public, owing in part to enthusiastic but not rapturous reviews; the most influential critic of the time, Clive Barnes of *The New York Times*, said, "If only good intentions were golden, *HAIR* would be great," although he did say it was "very much worth seeing." (Joseph Papp and Bernard Gersten had been concerned, Gersten says, when they saw Barnes fall asleep during the fairly raucous overture. That overture would be cut before *HAIR* opened on Broadway, though presumably not because of its soporific qualities.) However, Papp was not in a position to capitalize on its success. The show was scheduled to close on December 10, 1967, with Papp's deconstructed *Hamlet* starting previews just nine days later. If *HAIR* was to have any success beyond the eight-week run, it would need to find an audience somewhere other than the Anspacher Theater.

Enter Michael Butler, a well-connected aspiring politician with a habit of dating beautiful women (among them Audrey Hepburn and Candice Bergen) and

LEFT Michael Butler in 1968, not long after his fateful trip to see *HAIR* at the Public.

RIGHT Butler sent this memo to the *HAIR* cast and crew in 1969.

New York Shakespeare Festival PUBLIC THEATER *presents*

STEREO

HAIR
an american tribal love-rock musical

THE ORIGINAL CAST RECORDING

Produced by
JOSEPH PAPP
Book & Lyrics by
GEROME RAGNI & JAMES RADO
Music by
GALT MacDERMOT
Directed by
GERALD FREEDMAN
Setting by
MING CHO LEE
Costumes by
THEONI V. ALDREDGE
Lighting by
MARTIN ARONSTEIN
Musical Director
JOHN MORRIS
Associate Producer
BERNARD GERSTEN

PRS-319

SPECIAL COLLECTORS EDITION

LEFT The cover of the original off-Broadway cast recording, complete with superimposed photos of James Rado (bottom left) and Gerome Ragni (top right.)

TO: NEW YORK TRIBE MEMBERS

FROM: Michael Butler

RE: The Vietnam Moratorium Observance
Wednesday, October 15, 1969

A Confirmation of Our Mutual Agreement

In light of the fact that ours have been the only voices
in the American Theatre raised in objection to the Vietnam War
since October 1967, it seems an irony to silence our plea on the
very day when the eyes of the nation and the world will be focused
on this grievous problem.

Instead, we would like to continue to participate in significant fashion in the following manner:

Since, unfortunately, the strongest message in our society
is money, we will contribute the profits from the Wednesday evening, October 15 performance to any peace organization you choose.
Additionally I will contribute my royalty and Bertrand Castelli
will contribute his royalty. We will rely on the Company Peace
Chairman, Charles Lynch, to ask, jointly in our behalf, the other
creative talent to contribute their royalties as well. It is our
understanding that company members who can afford it will contribute whatever they can afford; and that Charles Lynch as Chairman
will make an appeal for one performance and/or day's salary to:
musicians, crew, theatre personnel, Hair office staff, press agents
and advertising agency.

-2-

All monies collected will be deposited in a Hair Peace
Account with Charles Lynch and I as co-signatories.

I am happy to serve as Charles's co-chairman and look
forward to your decision as to the disposition of the funds.
May I suggest that <u>all</u> those members of the Tribe who contribute
(crew, office staff, etc.) have an opportunity to vote on how
and where we spend the money?

Further, on October 15, we have mutually agreed to the
following:

   a. Cast participation in the Moratorium Rally at
      Bryant Park, Wednesday at 5:15; and the business-
      men's" rally at Hammarskjold Plaza (47th & Second
      Avenue) from 12:30-1:30 that day. I will provide
      buses to transport you to and from the rallies.

   b. Observance of one minute of silence within the
      production at the matinee and evening performances
      in all companies including foreign productions.

   c. Distribution of Mark Twain quote to our audience.

   d. Participation in the November 15 Washington, D.C. anti-
      Vietnam demonstration. This will be done by a full Hair
      Company complement either made up of representatives from

---

each Hair Company in the country or by the New York Company

with the understanding that the management will <u>not</u> be

penalized for the extra make-up performance whould we

close New York in order to participate in Washington.

   e. Placement of a Moratorium ad Wednesday, October 15 in

      the New York Times.

I am profoundly touched and more pleased than I can express,

that we are acting in accord toward what we hope will be a positive,

as well as significant effort for peace.

Yours in love and peace,

Michael Butler

an acute interest in Native Americans. It was this last interest that drew Butler, a scion of the family behind Butler Aviation as well as interests in real estate, to the Public Theater.

Playing on the "tribal" aspect of the musical's characters, an advertisement in the *Times* featured a photograph of five sage-looking Indians from a postcard that James Rado says he and Gerome Ragni had found in Vermont. (A subsequent poster, which was also used on the cover of the off-Broadway cast recording, showed a similar picture but with the torsos and heads of Rado and Ragni superimposed on two of the bodies.) "I thought it was an Indian show," says Butler, who had seen the ad while killing time at the New York Racquet Club between meetings. He had come to New York with Otto Kerner, the governor of Illinois and the head of the Kerner Commission on Civil Disorders; Butler became involved in Kerner's re-election campaign at the request of Robert F. Kennedy, a family friend.

He phoned Papp and asked for a copy of the *HAIR* poster. This was followed a few days later by a thick envelope from "International Sports Core, Oak Brook, IL," of which Butler was president. Inside the envelope were two Oak Brook Annuals, a brochure from Butler's polo club, and a request that the production be brought to Illinois; Butler himself was considering running for the U.S. Senate on an antiwar platform, and he hoped to treat his constituents to a command performance of *HAIR*. Butler also reached out to

another family friend, the veteran producer Roger L. Stevens, and requested a meeting with Papp.

Papp, who had a gift for cultivating wealthy donors to his various theatrical endeavors, quickly wrote back with a letter explaining the fiscal complexities of producing, and inviting Butler to lunch. The two soon began discussions about coproducing *HAIR*. Butler wasn't a complete neophyte in theatrical matters; he and his father had invested in such Stevens productions over the years as *West Side Story* and *The Golden Apple*. However, those were primarily investments. Butler's fervor for *HAIR* was far more personal and intense. "The reason I wanted to bring it to Illinois was my interest in ending the Vietnam War," he says. "I deeply wanted to get that message to the public."

As it happened, Butler wasn't the only person willing to put money into transferring *HAIR*—and the other offer was seemingly a safer bet. Burt Martinson, the chairman of the Public Theater's board, told Papp he would invest $50,000 to move the show to Henry Miller's Theater, one of the smaller Broadway venues. But Papp turned him down precisely because Martinson was so sympathetic to the Public and its mission. "Because the move was so speculative," Gersten says, "we reasoned that we wouldn't take money that would otherwise go to our work at the Public." While the terms of Butler's offer weren't as advantageous, it was essentially found money: If the Public didn't do business with him on *HAIR*, that money would vanish.

The Public would certainly benefit financially from *HAIR*—it received 1.5 percent of the gross from the Broadway and touring companies, and ultimately made more than $1.5 million. But these numbers would have been exponentially larger if it had accepted Burt Martinson's offer—and, of course, if the show in that incarnation had met with similar success. Several years later, in 1971, the Public reteamed with Galt MacDermot, this time with a musical adaptation of *The Two Gentlemen of Verona* as part of its Shakespeare in the Park season; it found its own benefactor to transfer the show to Broadway and claimed a much bigger percentage of the gross when it was a success. Within a year, Broadway would see three other shows make their way north from Papp's increasingly savvy institution.

(This self-sufficiency would soon prove even more lucrative when the Public premiered another new musical in 1975, this one also light on plot and also about a tight-knit company of young people. *A Chorus Line* became one of the very few musicals to prove even more popular than *HAIR*, generating approximately $40 million for the New York Shakespeare Festival.)

Butler's companion at that fateful first preview was Olivier Coquelin, who owned a handful of nightclubs in New York. After briefly considering moving *HAIR* to the Village Gate, a downtown nightclub that would soon host *Jacques Brel Is Alive and Well and Living in Paris*, he instead settled on one of Coquelin's clubs, Cheetah. Located on Broadway and 53rd Street, this club had a built-in clientele of the kind of young people Butler hoped to reach. The intermission was removed, and the curtain was moved from the conventional 8:30 to 7:30 p.m. so that patrons could attend the show and then, once the stage and seats were moved away, stay to dance at the club. (Post-show dancing would later become a more integrated part of the *HAIR* experience.)

Gerald Freedman returned from the Caribbean, where he had been directing Shakespeare, to restage the show before its reopening, a few days before Christmas.

NATOMA PRODUCTIONS--CHEETAH
"HAIR" Company

~~JONELLE ALLEN~~ 11
AD 4-0148

~~ED CROWLEY~~ 11
799-0121;PL 7-6300

~~STEVE CURRY~~ 10
CI 5-3990

~~WALKER DANIELS~~ 10
683-9387;LO 4-3250

STEVEN DEAN 11

over slept
GALE DIXON 15' 11
OR 9-9167

~~SALLY EATON~~ 11
677-8175

~~MARIJANE MARICLE~~ 11
PL 1-4379;PL 7-7676

JILL O'HARA 10
677-8183

~~ARNOLD WILKERSON~~ 11
TR4-7200

OLCOTT HOTEL
ROOM 616

~~SUSAN BATSON~~ 11
989-9763

~~LINDA COMPTON~~
SH 5-3232;SH 5-4983

SUZANNAH NORSTRAND
SH 5-3232

JANE LEVIN
TR 4-0321

ALMA ROBINSON
222-8561

~~WARREN BURTON~~ 25' left-
TE 8-7698   DOC
                   APPT.

THOMMIE BUSH
852-3879

WILLIAM HERTER
BU 8-0217;LO 4-3250

PAUL JABARA 15' 15 LAS
SH 8-8075

                   LATE 15'
B. J. JOHNSON
BU 7-4406

JIM MURPHY
628-7261;LO 4-3250

DAY WED DATE 20 DEC

PERFORMANCE NUMBER_____

PLEASE INITIAL   582-2970

REHEARSAL AT SHAKESPEARE
FESTIVAL

Posters for the transfer goosed the show's subtitle, calling it "The American Tribal Love-Rock Musical Smash!" It was billed as a coproduction between the Public and Michael Butler, who had invested $50,000—the exact same amount that Martinson had offered. And it was a total failure.

"We thought people would buy a ticket to *HAIR* and then stay to dance," Gersten says of the Cheetah strategy. "But the Cheetah people didn't come early and the *HAIR* people didn't follow it, and there was no reason to go on."

This version had its partisans. In *The Season,* a memorable book-length survey of the 1967–68 Broadway season, screenwriter William Goldman—who takes aim throughout at such sacred cows as Harold Pinter and Mike Nichols—shows a soft spot for the Cheetah *HAIR.* "It had youth and nice tunes and a terribly strong antiwar sentiment, and you didn't care (I didn't) that it was repetitive and silly. It was, for me, beyond criticism: I expect it is about the best theater I'll ever see in a discotheque." All the same, it closed on January 28 after just 45 performances, at which point the rights reverted to James Rado, Gerome Ragni, and Galt MacDermot.

Butler, who says now that "maybe the venue was an error," had gambled on *HAIR* and lost. And so he did what playboys and gamblers so often do—go double or nothing. Or, actually, quintuple or nothing: He reacquired the Broadway rights and raised an additional $250,000 for the Broadway transfer, $90,000 of which came from his father. He decided to abandon his planned run for the Senate and became a full-time producer. "Both the governor of Illinois and the mayor of Chicago, both of whom were my patrons, were stunned at my moving away from politics," Butler said. Later on, though, Charles Percy of Illinois, who was elected senator in 1967, told Butler, "You did more good with *HAIR* than you ever could have in the U.S. Senate."

For all the effort that the creators put into *HAIR* at the Public, Gersten credits Bulter for persevering with the show after anyone with any theatrical savvy would

LEFT A call sheet for a Cheetah performance, although rehearsals were still at the Public.

BELOW Paul Jabara, Suzannah Norstrand, Gerome Ragni, Steve Curry, Sally Eaton, and James Rado.

have cut his losses and walked away. "People always said, 'Oh, you gave up your rights.' We didn't give up our rights. It was dead as a doornail. And it took a naif like Michael Butler to bring in Tom O'Horgan and to bring in nudity. He lucked out. Or smarted out. Or both."

Accounts differ as to who exactly made the above decisions. Despite moving the Public production to Cheetah intact, Butler says he was eager to give *HAIR* a fresh look; he even told *The New York Times* on January 23 about his (unrealized) hope of having Alvin Ailey choreograph it on Broadway. "I felt it was too negative for what I was really interested in," he says, "and I also thought the director never smoked grass and didn't understand where we were coming from." (Butler was a strong believer in the liberating powers of marijuana. "A young gardener who was growing pot on my lower garden converted me," he says. "He was a pacifist, and he was drafted." Butler never found out what happened to the young man.)

The prospect of reopening the show in New York, a town that had already spurned one such transfer, motivated Butler to improve the material. "If it was just coming to Illinois," he says, "that would have been a different story. Also, the authors were very strong believers in changing the direction."

Rado agrees with Butler on this last count and only this last count; in fact, he maintains that he and Ragni are the only reason *HAIR* went through any sort of refurbishment on its way to Broadway. "When Michael Butler told us he didn't want a new director and a new production, that he wanted to just move the Cheetah production," he says, "we took our script and went elsewhere. It was a few weeks before Michael agreed to our terms." Among those terms: O'Horgan as the new director, new designers, new casting, and, most important, a new script with 13 new songs.

Regardless of who the motivating force was behind these extensive changes, the next step soon became clear—or as clear as anything can be in the labyrinthine history of *HAIR*. Tom O'Horgan, the off-off-Broadway trickster whom Rado and Ragni had approached almost a year earlier about directing their hippie musical, was about to apply his protean talents to taking an already adventurous musical and wrenching it even further from what Broadway was used to.

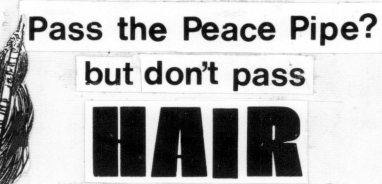

Pass the Peace Pipe?
but don't pass
HAIR

"A vivid uproar that has more wit, feeling and musicality than anything since "West Side Story"
–Newsweek

O'HORGAN'S METHODS

The casting continued until 12 days *after* opening night. More than a dozen songs were added. No theater had been secured until well into rehearsals. In short, little about *HAIR* followed any traditional sort of path on its accelerated trajectory from the failed Cheetah mounting to Broadway. This can be attributed to many factors: an unseasoned producer, the improvisatory ethos of the era, an amplified sound that deviated considerably from Broadway's acoustic status quo. But the single biggest X factor, the wildest card in an increasingly bizarre deck, was the selection of Tom O'Horgan as the director.

By 1971, O'Horgan would have four shows running on Broadway simultaneously—the other three were *Jesus Christ Superstar, Lenny*, and *Inner City*—plus a prominent New York production of his take on The Beatles' *Sgt. Pepper's Lonely Hearts Club Band*. In early 1968, though, he was an avowedly downtown director whose best-known piece was about a man in love with a pig. It was off-off-Broadway, most notably during his time at La MaMa, that he developed his own take on a new brand of "theater games." These were designed to break down any traditional barriers between the performer and his or her role, and the result was almost the opposite of the reality-at-all-costs hypernaturalism of Method acting, which had come into vogue a generation earlier. Instead, O'Horgan's techniques hinged on creating a new reality, one that would harness the energy of two dozen individual performers and funnel it into a malleable creative force.

As with so much of *HAIR*, these methods have been integrated so deeply into today's culture that it is difficult to grasp their import at the time. Perhaps the most dramatic example of this can be found in what have become known as "trust falls," those inhibition-shedding stalwarts of corporate retreats everywhere. O'Horgan employed an advanced version of this exercise, surrounding the designated "truster" with a circle of "trustees" and having him or her fall in any direction. In addition to any unconscious benefits that may have accrued from this particular exercise, it paved the way for one of O'Horgan's more striking visuals: Gerome Ragni's Berger leaping from a 9-foot- (2.7-meter-) high platform into the waiting arms of as few as four tribe members in the scene before "Going Down."

Other games were less risky but just as effective, according to cast members. Original cast member Natalie Mosco fondly remembers a rather nasty exercise in which the actors stood leaning slightly forward with their mouths open; the goal, she says, was to let one's jaw—and, by extension, one's entire body—relax to the point where saliva would pool and eventually drip to the ground. Another game, called "Journey," took the trust-fall notion to another level. A cast member would be blindfolded, hoisted into the air, and carried up, down and all over the theater. "We had Paul Jabara out a window horizontally at one point," Mosco says.

O'Horgan's loose, spontaneous style, one that encouraged the actors to experiment with their own movements, inflections, and even snippets of dialogue,

WHITE BOYS

White boys are so pretty
Skin as smooth as milk
White boys are so pretty
Hair like Chinese silk

White boys give me goose bumps
White boys give me chills
When they touch my shoulder
That's the touch that kills

My mother calls 'em lilies
I call 'em Piccadillies
My daddy warns me stay away
I say come on out and play

White boys are so groovy
White boys are so tough
Every time that they're near me
I just can't get enough

White boys are so pretty
White boys are so sweet
White boys drive me crazy
Drive me indiscreet

White boys are so sexy
Legs so long and lean
Love those sprayed-on trousers
Love the love machine

My brother calls 'em rubble
That's my kind of trouble
My daddy warns me "no no no"
But I say "white boys go go go"

White boys are so lovely
Beautiful as girls
I love to run my fingers
And toes through all their curls

Give me a tall
A lean
A sexy
A sweet
A pretty
A juicy
White boy

Black boys!
White boys!
Black boys!
White boys!

Mixed media!

LEFT The original "White Boys" singers were (from left) Emmeretta Marks, Melba Moore, and Lorrie Davis.

ABOVE Paul Jabara during rehearsals.

found its analogue in Julie Arenal's choreography, which also stemmed from group exercises. Steve Gillette, the show's lead guitarist, would sit in on rehearsals and jam—a marked departure from the standard practice of relying solely on piano accompaniment, often courtesy of the composer—and the company would start to dance. "What I'd then do was isolate individual moves from people and build a vocabulary," Arenal says. "And once I got four or five good moves, I put them on the rest of the company."

It is important not to assume, however, that this flexibility resulted in a loose or undisciplined staging. Cast member Marjorie Lipari stresses that any creative leeway for the actors was housed within an extremely codified structure. "Tom framed every beat with these beautiful images. It was sort of like, 'Movement-movement-movement-FRAME. Movement-movement-movement-FRAME.' There was precision, and it was choreographed, but it wasn't nailed to the floor. It was organic. It came out of our bodies."

Many directors and choreographers believe their work is most successful when it is least visible, when the audiences accept their actions and words as unforced. By that definition *HAIR* was nothing short of triumphant, especially when it came to Arenal's choreography—or dance direction, as it was ultimately credited. "In 1968, *Dance Magazine* asked me why there is no dancing in the show. Natural movement was not dancing to them. Other choreographers got it back then—Paul Taylor got it, for one—but not *Dance Magazine*." Slights of this nature would become commonplace in describing nearly every element of *HAIR*.

Ironically, the person who received perhaps the least guidance from O'Horgan was the actor at the play's center. "Tom only gave me one note the whole time," Rado says. "Everyone was dancing wildly during the 'White Boys' number, including myself, when at one point I stopped in my tracks and looked around at everybody else. Afterward, Tom came to me and said, 'When you stopped, that was good. It focused the scene.' That was the only note I ever got from Tom."

BLACK BOYS

Black boys are delicious
Mocha mousse, hot fudge
Maple syrup ladies
And brown sugar daddies
They are my dessert tray
When it comes to love

Once I tried a diet
Of quiet, rest, no sweets
But I went nearly crazy
And I went clearly crazy
Because I really craved for
My chocolate flavored treats

Black boys are nutritious
Black boys fill me up
Black boys are so damn yummy
They satisfy my tummy
Black boys are delicious
Raisins in sun
Black black black black
black black black black
Black boys

"Black Boys/White Boys"

After three white girls serenade Hud with a double-entendre-laden salute to chocolate treats, three black girls return the favor to Claude. "White Boys" came first at the Public, but the response to it was so ecstatic that the writers had to switch the two.

JAMES RADO: "'White Boys' was the first song we wrote for HAIR. When we finished it, we said, 'Hey, we can't have "White Boys" without another song called "Black Boys."'"

GALT MACDERMOT: "'White Boys' always stopped the show with Melba [Moore.] I don't think that has the same impact today—we're used to it. But originally we couldn't get the show going again."

THE CHANGES

Only about a third of the cast made the move from Cheetah to the Broadway production. Rado and Ragni came over, naturally. (Rado, who had only been a cast member at the Public for a matter of hours, officially took over as Claude.) Shelley Plimpton and Sally Eaton continued to play Crissy and Jeanie, and Linda Compton's pregnancy was the only thing that kept the Bay Ridge, Brooklyn trio of Compton, Paul Jabara, and Suzannah Evans (who had changed her name to Suzannah Norstrand) from moving intact.

As it happens, two cast members were pregnant during the Cheetah run. Eaton had told only a few people that she was pregnant at that point, and she was well into her second trimester when Rado asked her to audition for O'Horgan. "I toughed out the audition," she says, "though the dance portion was pretty grueling. I left feeling that Tom liked me and thought I was plucky." It was only then that the character of Jeanie became pregnant. Compton, who was a few weeks farther along than Eaton—and who gave birth on April 27, the opening night of *HAIR* on Broadway—went on to perform in various companies of the show for the next decade.

ABOVE It took some intervention from Michael Butler's father, but the Biltmore Theater finally gave Butler the Broadway house he needed.

RIGHT Diane Keaton, Melba Moore, Paul Jabara, and Ronnie Dyson at rehearsals.

LEFT Marjorie Lipari, Leata Galloway, and Lamont Washington.

"Easy to Be Hard"

Sheila lashes out at Berger after one self-centered and heartless act too many. This is arguably the first instance where the limitations of the tribe's devil-may-care attitude can be seen.

GALT MACDERMOT: *"This was done by a boy and two girls at first, and it didn't have anything to do with the plot. Where it is now makes much more sense. As a tune, it's a throwaway, but it's a great song and a great title."*

JAMES RADO: *"It was wonderful as a trio. It served as a sort of background for a scene. I'd like to see it go back there, maybe as a reprise. But it must stay as Sheila's song."*

EASY TO BE HARD

How can people be so heartless?
How can people be so cruel?
Easy to be hard
Easy to be cold

How can people have no feelings?
How can they ignore their friends?
Easy to be proud
Easy to say no

Especially people
Who care about strangers
Who care about evil
And social injustice
Do you only
Care about the bleeding crowd?
How about a needing friend?
I need a friend

How can people be so heartless?
You know I'm hung up on you
Easy to give in
Easy to help out

Especially people
Who care about strangers
Who say they care about social injustice
Do you only
Care about the bleeding crowd?
How about a needing friend?
I need a friend

How can people have no feelings?
How can they ignore their friends?
Easy to be hard
Easy to be cold
Easy to be proud
Easy to say no

LEFT Lynn Kellogg
(center) took on the
role of Sheila after Jill
O'Hara, the original
Sheila, joined the cast
of *George M!* rather than
transfer from the Public.

BELOW Steve Curry as Woof.

Eaton, meanwhile, gave birth three weeks after *HAIR* opened, surrounded by her fellow cast members in the office of the company physician, Dr. John Bishop. "I don't remember the full progression," Marjorie Lipari says, "but we were all in Dr. Bishop's office and sang 'Aquarius.' It was a stunning ritual." Eaton's baby would become a fixture backstage, as would Shelley Plimpton and Keith Carradine's infant daughter, Martha Plimpton (now a successful actress herself,) later in the run.

The rest of the Broadway company was assembled through a long series of auditions. In her memoir, *Letting Down My HAIR*, Lorrie Davis writes that rehearsals had already been going on for two days when she was hired. O'Horgan knew some of the actors from his La MaMa days: Lipari had toured Europe with O'Horgan's La MaMa troupe along with her twin brother, and Walter Michael Harris's family ran a children's theater that had relocated from Florida and become resident at La MaMa. Even so, Harris had no intention of auditioning for the show; he had only come to accompany a friend on guitar but recognized O'Horgan and agreed to try out himself.

The creators would later claim that many of the actors were plucked off the streets of Greenwich Village, but a great number of them were, while unseasoned, already working in their field. Davis had done a few television commercials; Melba Moore was a studio backup singer who had impressed MacDermot during a recording session; and Diane Keaton had recently graduated from the Neighborhood Playhouse, a prestigious

THE TRIBE NEIL "WOOF" DONOVAN

Conflicted Catholic, cut-up, and sidekick to Berger. Instructs Claude in how to avoid being drafted. Loves Mick Jagger.

A sort of genial sexual haze rests over the tribe, but Woof's hesitant (at first) crush on the Rolling Stones frontman is the only truly overt instance of homosexuality in the *HAIR* script. (Most directors opt for more explicit couplings during the staging.) Although he blatantly endorses only one of the five naughty words he sings about in "Sodomy"—"Masturbation / Can be fun"—Woof is clearly warming up to some or all of the other ones. "I don't think Woof is gay per se," says James Rado, who has described himself as "omnisexual" and who was in a longstanding romantic relationship with Gerome Ragni. "One thing that came through during the hippie movement was actual physical contact between men. You see that now, but you never did before—at least not in America—until the hippies started doing it."

actor-training school. (Moore and Keaton both declined to be interviewed for this book.)

Natalie Mosco and others describe going through four and even five rounds of auditions, including one in which the actors would each step forward from a circle and sing a cappella. Lipari auditioned after La MaMa's Ellen Stewart called her to say she had a premonition that Lipari would be cast; she remembers singing The Beatles' "If I Fell in Love With You" unaccompanied during her third audition—"and it was flawless." It was during that same audition that Rado rescued the woman who would become the best-known *HAIR* alumna. Diane Keaton had been dismissed with a group of other auditioners, and Rado remembers turning to Bertrand Castelli, Michael Butler's cosmopolitan executive producer, and saying, "Wait a minute. Call her back." Castelli darted over and grabbed her just before the elevator doors closed.

One cast member remained extremely involved with *HAIR*, at least by name, long after she had been left. Marti Whitehead only lasted three days in the company, but her name became shorthand that

LEFT In addition to shepherding *HAIR* through its later global expansion, Bertrand Castelli (seen here working with the cast in Munich, Germany) also played an instrumental role in casting perhaps the show's best-known original cast member.

RIGHT A series of Kenn Duncan photos of Diane Keaton, who left *HAIR* to star with Woody Allen in the play (and later film) *Play It Again, Sam*.

THE TRIBE JEANIE

Pregnant by someone she describes as "some crazy speed freak," although many directors have toyed with the idea that Claude is or at least might be the father. Frequently pops up (literally in the 1968 Broadway production, courtesy of a trap door) to spell out the relationships among the tribe members. Loves Claude.

"A pregnant Jeanie meant a complete departure from the runaway waif she'd been downtown," says Sally Eaton (shown right,) who arrived at Broadway rehearsals five months pregnant. "Jeanie could still be 'hung up' on Claude, but obviously he couldn't have fathered her child! As [executive producer] Bertrand Castelli...put it, 'that would make Claude look like a little shit.'

"My pregnancy moved Jeanie away from classic second-female-lead (soubrette/comedienne) into uncharted territory," Eaton continues. "Jeanie became a sort of sybil, speaking mostly to the audience, rarely onstage unless delivering a message. Where does Claude go when he becomes invisible? I think only Jeanie knows that."

Nina Dayton, who sold concessions in the back of the theater during *HAIR* as a teenager and went on to become the director of the show's archives, keeps a running checklist of common *HAIR* gaffes whenever she consults with new productions. One of the main ones involves Jeanie, who she feels is too often portrayed as a simpleton. In Claude's farewell to the tribe the night before he is inducted, "so many productions go into these long, tearful goodbyes," Dayton says. "But Jeanie is the only one who knows that they won't see him the next morning."

"HAIR"   OCT 4-68

"Don't Put It Down"

This mildly sarcastic paean to the American flag actually served as the opening number at the Public, where it was sung at different stages during the run by the two adults and by an otherworldly Apparition. On Broadway, despite Tom O'Horgan's insistence that the flag be folded according to military regulations, this song became a flash point for controversy throughout the show's run.

JAMES RADO: *"People treat this piece of cloth like a sacred object, and they thought it was sacrilegious. It is a pro-flag song, but we were also being playful. That was an irritant for some people, and sometimes it's wonderful to have that effect."*

GALT MACDERMOT: *"It was very badly sung originally [at the Public]. It wasn't country—it wasn't anything, really. It was originally sung as the opening number, and some people left right then. I think they just didn't like the singing."*

DIANE PAULUS (DIRECTOR OF THE 2009 REVIVAL): *"Something Jim said to me early on really stuck with me. He said, 'Hippies loved America. They had the American flag all over their clothes.' Then he said, 'Claude loves America so much that that's his problem.'"*

DON'T PUT IT DOWN

Om mane padme om
On mane padme om
Folding the flag means taking care of
the nation
Folding the flag is putting it to bed for
the night
I fell through a hole in the flag
I'm falling through a hole in the flag
Help!

Don't put it down
Best one around
Crazy for the red blue and white
Crazy for the red blue and white

You look at me
What do you see?
Crazy for the white red and blue
Crazy for the white red and blue

Cause I look different
You think I'm subversive
Crazy for the blue white and red
Crazy for the blue white and red

My heart beats true
For the red white and blue
Crazy for the blue white and red
Crazy for the blue white and red
And yellow fringe
Crazy for the blue white red and yellow

LEFT Although Steve Gamet, Steve Curry, and Gerome Ragni followed military protocol as they folded the flag, "Don't Put It Down" was a frequent source of criticism.

the fire department was in the theater. If the stage manager announced over the backstage loudspeaker, "Marti Whitehead, Marti Whitehead to the stage manager's desk," that was the signal for the actors to stop smoking anything they ought not be smoking.

An entirely new design team also came on board. Castelli had previously been the director of the Harkness Ballet in New York, where he had worked with set designer Robin Wagner as well as O'Horgan and Andy Warhol. He suggested Wagner, who had designed a handful of Broadway shows after working as an assistant to the legendary designers Ben Edwards and Oliver Smith, to work on *HAIR*; Wagner then enlisted Jules Fisher to design the lighting. (Wagner and Fisher, both still active, would go on to win 11 Tony Awards—and counting—between the two of them.) For costumes, Nancy Potts was hired on the strength of her work with the esteemed APA-Phoenix Repertory Company, where she had designed plays by everyone from Molière and Maxim Gorky to George Bernard Shaw and George M. Cohan.

The Public Theater carryovers had nearly as much memorization waiting for them as the new arrivals: Rado, Ragni, and MacDermot had used their "downtime" to create a mountain of new material. "When we got our script on the first day of rehearsal," says Natalie Mosco, "basically everything had been cut and rearranged." The relatively plotless incarnation of *HAIR* that ran at the Public consisted of some 20 songs in the space of two and a half hours. By the time it reached Broadway, the narrative at the Public had come to seem almost byzantine by comparison; O'Horgan found room for 13 new songs and cut only three of the old ones—all without any increase in the show's length.

Some of the changes involved merely shuffling the order of the songs. "Easy to Be Hard," originally sung in Act II by a trio of tribe members, was moved earlier and given to Sheila as a lament on the heels of Berger's callous treatment. The original director, Gerald Freedman, said he envisioned "Aquarius" as "a resurrection number" that came on the heels of Claude's mimed death; O'Horgan shifted it to the beginning, where it became a sort of generational overture. Freedman opted to begin the show with "Red, Blue and White," sung by the adult characters more or less sincerely; the song, ultimately renamed "Don't Put It Down," took on a more blatantly satiric edge and moved to near the end of the first act, just before "Frank Mills."

The most substantial musical changes to the score took place at the end. Gone were "Exanaplanetooch" and "The Climax," to say nothing of the tongue-in-cheek "Sentimental Ending" that intermittently found its way into the finale. In its place were "The Bed," which has likewise come and gone from the show over the years, and "Let the Sun Shine In," which is as deeply entrenched within the *HAIR* mystique as any song.

As before, Rado and Ragni would supply new ideas almost as quickly as they could scribble them down. Luckily, they had in MacDermot a collaborator who could keep pace with these two fertile imaginations. "If I don't get it that morning, I quit," MacDermot says of his writing style. "If it doesn't come fast, it means it's no damn good." He was incredibly faithful to his cowriters, setting to music exactly what he received. One line in the song "The Climax," which was cut after the Cheetah run, reflects just how unquestioning MacDermot was. "I had scrawled 'funny but by the end bitter and serious and deadly' at the bottom of the page as a stage direction," Rado says. "And when Galt played the song for us, it was there as part of the lyric! We liked, so we kept it."

Other, equally consequential changes were devoted to the overall tone, nearly always moving the mood in a lighter direction. Two adult actors had played Claude's parents as well as the other establishment roles at the Public, while O'Horgan fragmented these characters into campy trios, with men often playing women and vice versa. By scaling back the Claude-Berger-Sheila love triangle, O'Horgan turned *HAIR* more decisively into the story of a tribe. These three characters are still the central players, with Woof, Hud, Jeanie, and Crissy also playing notable roles, but the demarcation between lead and supporting characters is much less pronounced.

O'Horgan also dispensed with Freedman's final image of toy tanks and machine guns sputtering on an empty stage as the lights dimmed. "I think that's an eloquent way of stating the futility of war," William Goldman wrote of the original finale in *The Season*. O'Horgan would empty the stage for his own somber finale—but only after a rousing rendition of "Let the Sun Shine In" and before an even more effervescent full-cast performance of the song "Hair."

Rado declines to specify which textual contributions are his and which are Ragni's. "Jerry said to me years later, 'Don't tell people who wrote what,' and I never have," he says. "But it's very much 50/50." However, other cast members have suggested that 50 percent is too high a number for either of the two men. With so much improvisation taking place in the rehearsal room, many participants feel their own contributions were absorbed into the final script without sufficient recognition.

In *Letting Down My HAIR*, Lorrie Davis writes how she created Abe Lincoln's Gettysburg Address rap in Act II almost in its entirety, right down to the doo-wop background. Much of the cast was angry, she wrote, that their collective contributions to the script, "separately small, but large when combined," were never credited. "Jonathan Kramer and Paul Jabara and Sally Eaton and myself put the most stuff in there," Davis says today, "and we never even got a thank you." Original cast member Robert I. Rubinsky agrees with this overall assessment: "I mean, I only added a little twist or interpretation—I think it was my thing to make the principal a Nazi. But a lot of people actually wrote words." (Similar accusations would surround *A Chorus Line*, which used even more interrogative methods to develop its narrative.)

Rado maintains that these contributions were confined to the staging. "We allowed a lot of freedom from the actors and director. The scenes were up for grabs, in a sense. The lyrics, however, were not. We had to constantly keep our eyes and ears peeled for excesses."

Well into rehearsals, however, the cast had more pressing matters to worry about than who wrote what. For one thing, they didn't have a theater. Just as the old guard of producers wanted no part of *HAIR* when Rado and Ragni shopped it around, Michael Butler was meeting with resistance from the owners of every Broadway theater. Mosco describes rehearsals frequently stopping as Butler would enter the studio with various well-dressed theater owners. Everyone would stop what they were working on, she says, and jump to the Be-In scene, usually starting with Shelley Plimpton singing "Frank Mills."

ABOVE Jonathan Kramer at rehearsals in 1968.

LEFT Michael Butler hard at work.

ABOVE Butler with two fellow peace activists, Gloria Steinem and William Sloane Coffin.

RIGHT Clutching flowers for the imminent Be-In, Crissy (Allison Case) on Broadway in 2010 pauses to sing "Frank Mills."

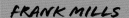

FRANK MILLS

I met a boy called Frank Mills
On September twelfth right here
In front of the Waverly
But unfortunately
I lost his address

He was last seen with his friend,
A drummer, he resembles George Harrison of the Beatles
But he wears his hair
Tied in a small bow at the back

I love him but it embarrasses me
To walk down the street with him
He lives in Brooklyn somewhere
And wears this white crash helmet

He has gold chains on his leather jacket
And on the back are written the names
Mary
And Mom
And Hell's Angels

I would gratefully
Appreciate it if you see him tell him
I'm in the park with my girlfriend
And please

Tell him Angela and I
Don't want the two dollars back
Just him!

"Frank Mills"

Crissy, thus far an ever-present but fairly silent figure, steps forward and sings this quiet ballad about the guy who may have gotten away—if she ever really had him to begin with.

GALT MACDERMOT: *"The first night, there was no applause. The second night, it was the first applause of the whole show. It was a letter in the Village Voice, I was told. It's a beautiful song. I had to plead with Gerry Freedman to keep it in the show."*

JAMES RADO: *"I learned a funny thing not that long ago. 'Frank Mills' stemmed from a letter to the editor in the Village Voice. I was so moved by the letter. I showed it to Jerry, and it became a Crissy speech that turned into a song. But a year or two ago, a journalist showed me a British rock magazine from early 1967. It had personal ads in the back, and several of the ads had one line or another from that letter. Somebody at the Village Voice had mixed them all together and made a fake letter out of them!"*

ABOVE The "Black Boys/ White Boys" sequence would have been a showstopper anyway, but Nancy Potts's conjoined girl-group gown for the "White Boys" trio certainly helped.

LEFT Steve Gillette, the show's lead guitarist, would often come to rehearsals and improvise as a way of generating new movements from the cast. Seen here with him are Curry, Ragni, and Kellogg.

But the Shuberts and the Nederlanders (who between them owned a majority of the Broadway houses) both passed on *HAIR*. It took an intervention on the part of Butler's father to convince the theater owner David Cogan to offer the Biltmore, which almost never housed musicals but had become unexpectedly available when the New York premiere of Joe Orton's *Loot* closed that March after just 22 performances.

Once the Biltmore had been chosen, Fisher and Wagner had only four days to load in the sets and lights. Musicals typically place more intricate technical demands on a theater than plays, and despite its loose structure and anything-goes spirit, *HAIR* had an extremely complicated lighting design. Despite having only two-thirds of the lighting capacity of most Broadway musicals at his disposal, given the Biltmore's reputation as a non-musical venue, Fisher came up with an enormous array of visual effects. The "Walking in Space" sequence alone had more than 100 lighting cues, with three technicians using every available hand, foot, elbow, and knee to work all of the levers. Another sequence employed what he called a "light organ," which went to the opposite extreme: A button would be pushed, Fisher says, and "all of a sudden, the lighting would respond to the frequencies of the music for two minutes at a time."

Wagner, meanwhile, created a completely exposed playing area, with the wings and radiator pipes and even stagehands visible. Rado had asked that the stage have a steep "rake," or slope upward away from the audience, so that the actors' feet would be more visible; Wagner incorporated the resulting prominence of the floor into his design by stenciling graffiti on it. The main scenic element was a massive tower of scaffolding far upstage that housed various bits of hippie bric-a-brac: a neon sign for the Waverly movie theater, a jukebox, a large "third eye," and often a few gyrating actors. One other unusual item could also be found on the stage: the band. MacDermot had nearly doubled the size of his orchestra, from five members to nine, and it now performed in a hollowed-out truck onstage as opposed to in the traditional subterranean pit.

Compared with the frantic efforts of Fisher and Wagner, Potts had a relatively luxurious three weeks to design the costumes. The actors went to the APA-Phoenix Theater costume shop and were free to pick more or less whatever they wanted; the costume shop would frequently dye or distress the clothes to make them look grungier than they were. Some people wore the same clothes at each performance; others liked to mix things up. The notable exception to this loose aesthetic came in the song "White Boys." Potts designed an enormous (size 60) fuschia sequined tube dress that looked at first like three separate floor-length gowns, the sort that the members of a 1960s girl group like the Supremes might wear. The trio of singers began the song standing right up against one another, and it wasn't until the second chorus, when they moved apart, that the audience realized it was just one dress.

Once everyone on either side of the footlights had acclimated to their new home, one last ritual remained before the Biltmore was truly ready for *HAIR*. Walter Michael Harris says he and some of his fellow cast members evaded the security guards the night before opening and had what he calls "an all-night vigil" to prepare the theater "through prayer, meditation, singing, and some consciousness-raising herb. … It was utterly sincere—our attempt to purify the space."

Probably no other musical in Broadway history has gone through as drastic an upheaval in as little time. A total of 13 new songs were written, and in less than three months, the show was restaged, recast, rechoreographed, and redesigned (sets, costumes, and lighting.) Perhaps most important for its long-term success, however, was the innovation that came at the end of Act I: an addition but, more crucially, a subtraction. When quotes began surfacing in the media about how scandalous the show was, they were not referring to the occasional vulgarities or the prevalent haze of (not always artificial) marijuana smoke. They were referring to the nude scene.

RIGHT A mirror-image negative of Curry's impressive head became the iconic poster image.

BELOW "The Bed" being performed in 1968.

THE BED

Oh the bed
Oooh the bed
Ahhh the bed
Oh the bed
Mmmm the bed
I love the bed

You can lie in bed
You can lay in bed
You can die in bed
You can pray in bed
You can live in bed
You can laugh in bed
You can give your heart
Or break your heart in half
in bed

You can tease in bed
You can please in bed
You can squeeze in bed
You can freeze in bed
You can sneeze in bed
Catch the fleas in bed
All of these
Plus eat crackers and cheese
in bed

Oh the bed is a thing
Of feather and spring
Of wire and wood
Invention so good

Oh the bed comes complete
With pillow and sheet
With blanket electric
And breath antiseptic

Let there be sheets
Let there be beds
Foam rubber pillows
Under our heads

Let there be sighs
Filling the room
Scanty pajamas
By Fruit of the Loom

You can eat in bed
You can beat in bed
Be in heat in bed
Have a treat in bed
You can rock in bed
You can roll in bed
Find your cock in bed
Lose your soul in bed

You can lose in bed
You can win in bed
But never never never never
Never never never never
Never never never
Never can you sin in bed!

"The Bed"

The tribe breaks into a riotous list of all the things you can do in bed, from squeezing to freezing to giving your heart to losing your soul, as Claude and Sheila make love. The seduction originally took place via Claude's song "Exanaplanetooch," followed by Sheila's "The Climax"; neither of these songs made it to opening night on Broadway. As with many productions, "The Bed" was not in the 2009 revival.

JAMES RADO: *"I don't miss it, although I loved the way it was done in the Broadway version. If that number is done right, it can be super-exuberant. It takes things up to a new frenzy, a big kind of orgiastic moment."*

MICHAEL BUTLER PRESENTS
HAIR
THE AMERICAN TRIBAL LOVE-ROCK MUSICAL
BOOK & LYRICS: GEROME RAGNI, JAMES RADO/MUSIC: GALT MAC DERMOT
EXECUTIVE PRODUCER: BERTRAND CASTELLI/DIRECTED BY: TOM O'HORGAN

THE NUDE SCENE

During the three years that Rado and Ragni spent amassing the experiences and ideas that would become *HAIR*, they attended a Central Park be-in at which two men spontaneously stripped and stood in the crowd naked. Accounts vary about the fate of these two anonymous men; some remember them as having been arrested, while others maintain that the appreciative crowd created a barrier between them and the police that allowed them to put their clothes back on and vanish. Either way, the image lingered in the two writers' minds. They attempted to replicate it in a nude scene that they had written for the Public production of *HAIR*, one that would just include two male actors, but Papp vetoed the idea. That was the end of that…until the first preview at the Biltmore on April 11, 1968, when Ragni, Curry, and Gamet stood naked at the climax of the Act I Be-In sequence.

This act has been depicted as a spontaneous act of liberation, but the reality appears to be far more premeditated. Clive Barnes, *The New York Times* critic

ABOVE Steve Gamet was one of the first three people to stand naked at the Act I finale.

RIGHT The other two were Gerome Ragni and Steve Curry.

WHERE DO I GO

Where do I go?
Follow the river
Where do I go?
Follow the gulls

Where is the something
Where is the someone
That tells me why I live and die?

Where do I go?
Follow the children
Where do I go?
Follow their smiles

Is there an answer
In their sweet faces
That tells me why I live and die?

Follow the wind song
Follow the thunder
Follow the neon in young lovers' eyes

Down to the gutter
Up to the glitter
Into the city
Where the truth lies

Where do I go?
Follow my heartbeat
Where do I go?
Follow my hand

Where will they lead me
And will I ever
Discover why I live and die?

Why do I live? (beads, flowers)
Why do I die? (freedom, happiness)
Tell my why (beads, flowers)
Tell me where (freedom, happiness)
Tell my why (beads, flowers)
Tell me why (freedom!)

"Where Do I Go?"

Claude, torn about whether to stay with his friends or risk his life in Vietnam, ponders why he lives and dies. He is finally joined by the rest of the tribe, who have shed their clothes and stand naked on all sides of him.

GALT MACDERMOT: *"This was one of the first songs we wrote. It's a beautifully written lyric."*

JAMES RADO: *"Joe Papp wanted to cut it. I can sort of understand why, but it gave me a complex about doing the song."*

whose enthusiastic response to the Public Theater production provided much of the momentum for a Broadway transfer, once recalled that Bertrand Castelli had mentioned over a drink that a nude scene was being planned and that the attendant publicity would work to the show's advantage. Michael Butler said he first learned of the possibility from O'Horgan: "It was Tom's basic idea, and I said, 'Fine.'"

Castelli and Butler had done their research before agreeing to such an event. "They looked it up," Rado recalls, "and found a law on the books that said nudity was legal if it was in a tableau, with no movement." The presence of naked bodies was only actionable if these bodies were to start moving. (The law did not differentiate between minors—a category that included several cast members—and adults.) So O'Horgan had the tribe untie a parachute-like background scrim from its batten and then ritualistically spread it across the stage and over a table. Slits had been cut into the scrim, and while Claude sang "Where Do I Go?" atop the table, the actors disrobed underneath the scrim; they would then rise up through the slits and stand stock still as Jules Fisher's lights projected a Robin Wagner-designed floral pattern from directly overhead for about 20 seconds. As soon as the lights went out, the actors scurried offstage.

The murky lighting was "a totally artistic decision," Fisher says. "The brightness level was related to what was right emotionally at that moment, not to public mores." Nonetheless, the response was every bit as explosive as Castelli had anticipated, with binoculars and flash cameras appearing on a nightly basis. O'Horgan even played into this furor on opening night by capping the scene with a fake police bust, complete with flashing lights and two policemen—actually company members—appearing in the orchestra and threatening to put the entire audience under arrest. The "raid" became part of the established script, and Rado and Ragni themselves would go on to play the two policemen during the short-lived 1977 Broadway revival of *HAIR*. (The raid did not appear in the 2009 revival, which instead uses the sound of police sirens as the actors leave the stage—with the lights still on.)

This gag illustrates the ambivalence that came with the inclusion of the nude scene. The creators have insisted repeatedly that the scene is crucial to the musical's messages of love and the shedding of inhibitions, and O'Horgan had used nudity in similar ways off-off-Broadway. (To a lesser degree, so had Freedman, at New York City Opera.) That said, nobody involved with *HAIR* denies the effect it had on the show's popularity. "I have to thank the nude scene for getting a lot of people into the theater," Butler says. "That was the end of the first act, and then we had them for the second act, which is when the antiwar message was really laid out for them."

As for the policemen joke—which first implicates and then exonerates the audience of voyeurism, adding a frisson of lawlessness—this was hardly the only acknowledgement of the scene's inherent titillation factor. *Playboy* magazine photographed several of the actresses on more than one occasion; newspaper advertisements marking the show's second anniversary on Broadway featured a photo of the cast standing in a row wearing only a sash covering their midsections that said "What else would you wear on your 2nd birthday!"

For every defender who hailed the freedom exemplified in the Be-In scene, there was also a detractor who cried "commercialism." In *The Season*, William

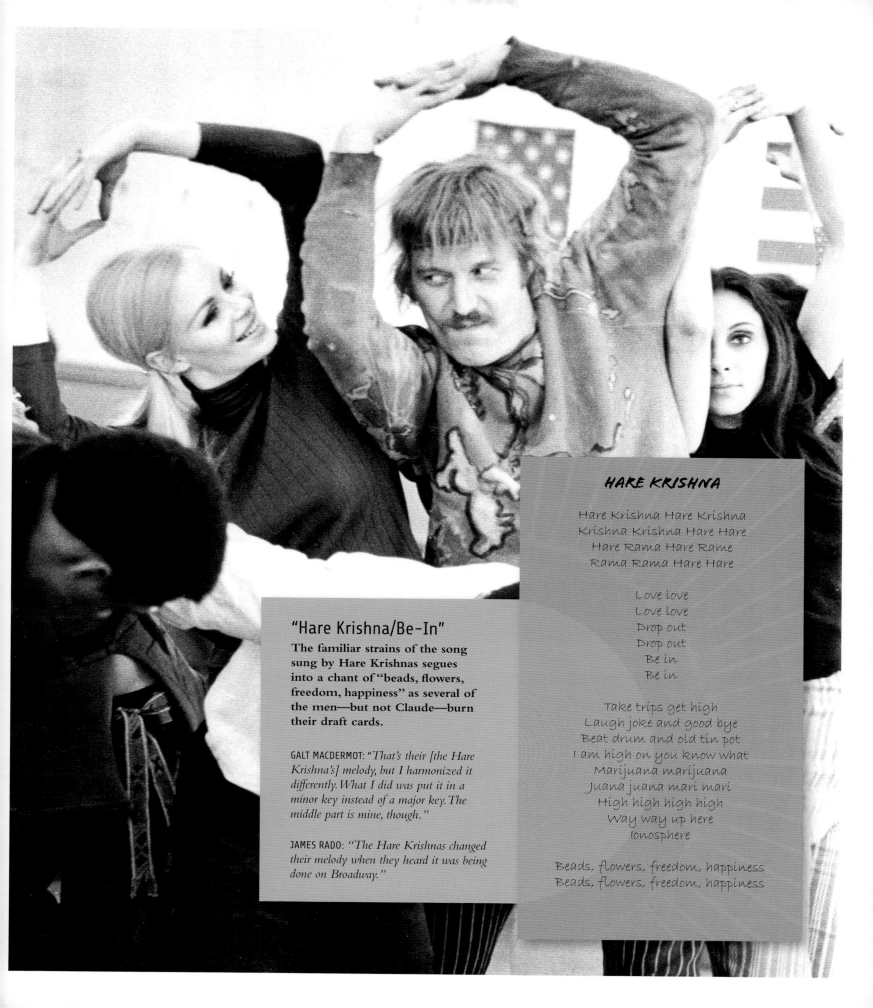

"Hare Krishna/Be-In"

The familiar strains of the song sung by Hare Krishnas segues into a chant of "beads, flowers, freedom, happiness" as several of the men—but not Claude—burn their draft cards.

GALT MACDERMOT: *"That's their [the Hare Krishna's] melody, but I harmonized it differently. What I did was put it in a minor key instead of a major key. The middle part is mine, though."*

JAMES RADO: *"The Hare Krishnas changed their melody when they heard it was being done on Broadway."*

HARE KRISHNA

Hare Krishna Hare Krishna
Krishna Krishna Hare Hare
Hare Rama Hare Rame
Rama Rama Hare Hare

Love love
Love love
Drop out
Drop out
Be in
Be in

Take trips get high
Laugh joke and good bye
Beat drum and old tin pot
I am high on you know what
Marijuana marijuana
Juana juana mari mari
High high high high
Way way up here
Ionosphere

Beads, flowers, freedom, happiness
Beads, flowers, freedom, happiness

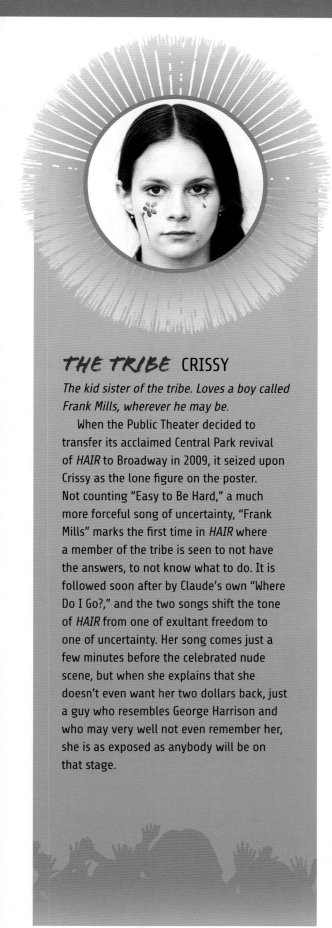

THE TRIBE CRISSY

The kid sister of the tribe. Loves a boy called Frank Mills, wherever he may be.

When the Public Theater decided to transfer its acclaimed Central Park revival of *HAIR* to Broadway in 2009, it seized upon Crissy as the lone figure on the poster. Not counting "Easy to Be Hard," a much more forceful song of uncertainty, "Frank Mills" marks the first time in *HAIR* where a member of the tribe is seen to not have the answers, to not know what to do. It is followed soon after by Claude's own "Where Do I Go?," and the two songs shift the tone of *HAIR* from one of exultant freedom to one of uncertainty. Her song comes just a few minutes before the celebrated nude scene, but when she explains that she doesn't even want her two dollars back, just a guy who resembles George Harrison and who may very well not even remember her, she is as exposed as anybody will be on that stage.

Goldman questioned the motives behind the nudity: "It added nothing to the show, no matter how much the creative hierarchy pleaded artistic purity." Putting aside any discussion of decency and pornography (although these would resurface as productions of *HAIR* began to open elsewhere in the country,) similar objections on aesthetic grounds would continue to dog the production.

Once the nude scene became a central part of *HAIR* lore, new actors auditioning to join one of the show's many companies were well aware of it. This, however, was not the case for the original cast members, many of whom found themselves being lobbied to participate in a new and potentially unsettling situation. Amy Saltz, who was the assistant to director Gerald Freedman at both the Public and Cheetah, remembers being visited by a handful of the actors who had moved with the show to Broadway, which included Paul Jabara and Suzannah Norstrand, early in previews. "They were being asked to do the nude scene, and they didn't want to do it," Saltz says. "They said Jerry Ragni was putting a ton of pressure on them and saying, 'You're not being cool,' and this and that."

After first threatening to hire "ringers"—strippers and other performers unconcerned with appearing naked on stage—the producers ultimately agreed to pay each cast member an additional $1.50 per performance if they took their clothes off. And the nudity was not compulsory—at least not for the original performers. (Marjorie Lipari, for one, never did the nude scene, although she says she was more concerned about being naked in front of the stagehands. Instead, she helped spread the scrim out.) Like so many other aspects of *HAIR*, the scene evolved through a combination of idealism and business savvy, of what must be said and what could be sold.

OPPOSITE TOP The original Broadway cast perform the nude scene.

ABOVE LEFT Shelley Plimpton, the original Crissy.

BELOW The nude scene in a later production.

OPPOSITE BOTTOM In July 1970 the cast of *Hair* performed for the World Youth Assembly, a group of 750 young people selected by the United Nations. The profits from an earlier performance also went to the group.

THE STORY

With each iteration of *HAIR*, the text would change and morph until Rado and Ragni were told it could not change any further. Joseph Papp reached the point where he would tear up the voluminous pages of suggestions without looking at them. Michael Butler locked the two stars out of the Biltmore Theater after one or two "embellishments" too many. Even after the 2009 revival had opened to rave reviews, Rado seemed disinclined to close the door entirely on revisions: "It should stop changing—in a way. The new version on Broadway is almost perfect. There are a few things I might think of…" Sure enough, when a new tribe replaced the old one in March 2010, Rado had a handful of rewrites at the ready.

This resistance to solidifying *HAIR* meant that a true script didn't even exist until Actors' Equity finally demanded one well into the original run, at which point production stage manager Fred Reinglas spent two days typing up a transcription. Pocket Books published a script in September 1969, but it was cobbled together from various versions and does not reflect one that was ever actually performed.

Here, then, is a description of what was presented on opening night at the Biltmore on April 29, 1968. Any changes in the song list for the 2009 revival have been noted; variations in the staging and the script have not.

ACT I

As the audience enters, the cast is staggered throughout the theater: on the stage, in the balconies, on the scaffolding, and in the orchestra. The only constant is the character of Claude, who sits silent and cross-legged on the stage. A small fire chalice is placed before him, and as the cast begins moving in slow motion toward the stage, Sheila and Berger ritualistically cut off a lock of Claude's hair and, in a symbolic foreshadowing of his fate, sacrifice it to the fire.

Once the rest of the tribe has gathered on stage in a circle, one of its members leads the rest in hailing the age of "Aquarius," one in which "peace will guide the planets / And love will steer the stars." The song ends with the striking of a gong, and the tribe breaks apart to reveal the limitlessly liberated Berger. After proclaiming the spiritual side of love, introducing himself, and stripping down to an Indian loincloth, he heads off the stage and into the laps of the audience before singing about a 16-year-old virgin named "Donna" for whom he has been searching. This song includes Berger mounting a scaffold and swinging over the audience's heads on a rope.

Then begins a fairly quick sequence of briefer songs as the tribe breaks into smaller pockets around the stage. First is "Hashish," a paean to various mind-bending substances, including cocaine and LSD. The tribe members quickly reconfigure into various religious tableaux, and the Catholic-raised Woof sings

TOP The "psychedelic teddy bear" Berger.

ABOVE Ron Williams as Hud and Elke Koska as Sally in the Munich production of *HAIR*.

RIGHT An original Playbill from the Biltmore Theater.

Biltmore Theatre

PLAYBILL
the national magazine for theatregoers

HAIR
I

BILTMORE THEATRE

MICHAEL BUTLER

presents

The Natoma Production of

HAIR
The American Tribal Love-Rock Musical

| *Book and Lyrics by* | *Music by* |
| GEROME RAGNI & JAMES RADO | GALT MacDERMOT |

| *Executive Producer* | *Directed by* |
| BERTRAND CASTELLI | TOM O'HORGAN |

| *Dance Director* | *Musical Director* |
| JULIE ARENAL | GALT MacDERMOT |

| *Costumes by* | *Scenery by* | *Lighting by* | *Sound by* |
| NANCY POTTS | ROBIN WAGNER | JULES FISHER | ROBERT KIERNAN |

with

STEVE CURRY	RONALD DYSON	SALLY EATON	LEATA GALLOWAY
PAUL JABARA	DIANE KEATON	LYNN KELLOGG
JONATHAN KRAMER	MELBA MOORE	SHELLEY PLIMPTON
JAMES RADO	GEROME RAGNI	LAMONT WASHINGTON

and

Donnie Burks	Lorri Davis	Steve Gamet
Walter Harris	Hiram Keller	Marjorie LiPari
Emmaretta Marks		Natalie Mosco
Suzannah Norstrand		Robert I. Rubinsky

17

MUSICAL NUMBERS
ACT I.

Aquarius	Ron and Company
Donna	Berger and Company
Hashish	Company
Sodomy	Woof and Company
Colored Spade	Hud and Company
Manchester	Claude and Company
Ain't Got No	Woof, Hud, Dionne, and Company
I Believe In Love	Sheila
Air	Jeanie, Crissy, Dionne and Company
Initials	Company
I Got Life	Claude and Company
Going Down	Berger and Company

27

Who's Who in the Cast

JAMES RADO (*Claude*) has appeared on Broadway in *Lion in Winter* and *Luther*, off Broadway in *The Knack, The Infantry*, and *Hang Down Your Head and Die*.

GEROME RAGNI (*Berger*) who originated the role of Berger in the Public Theatre production of *Hair*, appeared on Broadway in *Hamlet* and off Broadway in *Viet Rock, The Knack* and *Hang Down Your Head and Die*. He is a member of the Open Theatre and has appeared off off Broadway at Cafe La Mama.

LYNN KELLOGG (*Sheila*)—This is a Broadway début for Miss Kellogg. She has appeared on television with Johnny Carson, Merv Griffin and Mike Douglas, the Today show and The Bitter End. She toured Vietnam with the USO show starring Jonathan Winters.

STEVE CURRY (*Woof*) has had leading roles in the Broadway productions of *Gypsy, I Can Get It For You Wholesale, West Side Story* (as Baby John and Arab) and *Camelot* with Richard Burton. He has recently returned from Vietnam where he starred in, produced, directed, and toured his own complete variety show.

LAMONT WASHINGTON (*Hud*) attended the High School of Performing Arts and started his acting career off

Broadway in *Once Upon An Island*. On Broadway he was stand-in for Sammy Davis, Jr. in *Golden Boy* and played the part thirty-two times. He has sung with Count Basie's band, and on television has performed in *Call Back* and *The New Yorkers*.

SALLY EATON (*Jeanie*) was born in Great Lakes, Illinois under the sign of Aries. She grew up in Warren, Pennsylvania, "the conformity capital of the United States." She has spent the last three years on the lower East Side of New York watching the hippie movement take shape. She is for acid, sex and peace.

MELBA MOORE (*Dionne*) is a native of New York. This is her Broadway début. She has sung at the Concord Hotel, Grossinger's, and the Rat Fink Room. On television she has appeared on the special, *Comedy Is King*, starring Alan King.

SHELLEY PLIMPTON (*Crissy*)— Shelley is making her Broadway début in *Hair*, and was working as a cashier when the producers of *Hair* discovered her.

RONALD DYSON (*Ron*)—This is Mr. Dyson's Broadway début. He is a native of Washington, D.C. and made his singing début in 1954 at the Brooklyn Academy of Music in *Startime*.

34

"Donna"

Berger is introduced through a frenetic tale of his search for a virginal beauty, one that in his imagination has taken him from San Francisco to India to South America.

JAMES RADO: *"We were off for lunch during rehearsals at the Public, and we met this older hippie. He had a cane made out of a tree branch inlaid with precious stones and various icons from his travels, and he launched into a story about how he was looking for this 16-year-old with tattoos who had been arrested because she was so beautiful. We went back to the theater and wrote it all down."*

GALT MACDERMOT: *"I wrote 'Donna' originally for Claude—well, for Jim—but it's really Berger's song. It goes through different fields, but it's always fast."*

WILL SWENSON (BERGER IN THE 2009 REVIVAL): *"I think Donna is a sort of manifestation of Berger's journey for the constant party. Luckily, you can justify a lot of the lyrics—and I don't think this is a cop-out—by the fact that he's probably high at any given point."*

DONNA

Oh
Once upon a looking-for-Donna-time
There was a sixteen-year-old virgin
Oh Donna oh oh Donna oh oh oh
Looking for my Donna

I just got back from looking for Donna
San Francisco
Psychedelic urchin
Oh Donna oh oh Donna oh oh oh
Looking for my Donna

Have you seen
My sixteen-year-old tattooed woman?
Heard a story
She got busted for her beauty oh oh oh
Oh oh!

Once upon a looking-for-Donna-time
I'm never going to end my searchin'
Oh Donna oh oh Donna oh oh oh
Looking for my Donna

I've been to India and saw the yogi light
In South America the Indian smoke glows bright
I'm reincarnated and so are we all
And in this lifetime we'll rise
Before we fall
Before we fall

Once upon a looking-for-Donna-time
Hope my heart don't need no surgeon
Oh Donna oh oh Donna oh oh oh
Looking for my Donna

And I'm gonna to show her
Life on earth can be sweet
Gonna lay my mutated head at her feet
And I'm gonna love her make love to her
Till the sky turns brown
I'm evolving I'm evolving
Through the drugs
That you put down

Once upon a looking-for-Donna-time
There was a sixteen-year-old virgin
Oh Donna oh oh Donna oh oh oh
Looking for my Donna
Looking for my Donna

Donna!

a hymn-like tribute to "Sodomy" and other ostensibly perverse acts. Two white members then carry in a black man named Hud, who rattles off a series of racial epithets in "Colored Spade."

As Hud sings, Claude is being "tarred" (with mud) and feathered by three of the women, who then wash him clean. He is wearing a British flag for a loincloth, and he affects a North Country accent as he tells the audience that he's from "Manchester England" and not Flushing, Queens.

Hud and Woof are joined by Dionne, and the three lead the tribe in listing the sacrifices inherent to the hippie lifestyle in "Ain't Got No;" among the things denied them are homes, shoes, pot, and faith. This definition through denial gives way to the more affirming "I Believe in Love," which Sheila sings after arriving as if on horseback and before leading the tribe in a chant for peace. The final main cast member, Jeanie, pops up from a trapdoor to sing "Air," a sardonic ditty about the environment. She emerges completely from the hole to reveal that she's pregnant—and not by Claude, whom she loves.

Three sets of mothers and fathers insult their collective son, Claude, for his "disgusting" clothes and present him with his draft notice. When his mother demands to know what he has that makes him so superior, he responds with "I Got Life." The tribe then pokes fun at the depersonalization of language through "Initials," a hodgepodge of phrases and names made of three-letter initials.

Again in triplicate, a group of fascist school principals in Hitler mustaches berate Berger for violating the school's dress code. Berger leaps from the scaffolding into the waiting arms of his friends before singing "Going Down," with its mix of sexual innuendo and references to a Miltonian fall from Heaven.

The news of Berger's expulsion is met with worse news, as Claude informs the tribe that he has passed his army physical and will soon be inducted. Before the tribe can process this, a tourist couple emerges from the audience to ask Claude and Berger about their long hair; Claude's response is the song "Hair." The female member of the couple (whose name has subsequently been changed to Margaret Mead) sings "My Conviction," an anthropological interpretation of why the male is emerging from his drab camouflage. Upon departing, she opens her long coat to show that she's actually a man in drag.

Sheila reappears as the tribe sings "Sheila Franklin." She is back from an antiwar rally in Washington, D.C., where she bought Berger a yellow satin shirt. But the impulsive, unappreciative Berger accuses her of jealousy and tears up the shirt, spurring Sheila to sing "Easy to Be Hard," about the cruelty of so many people toward others. Claude attempts to console Sheila, which prompts Jeanie to reemerge from the trapdoor and, in the space of 61 words, deliver approximately half of the show's plot:

"This is the way it is. Sheila's hung up on Berger. I'm hung up on Claude. Claude is hung up on a cross over Sheila and Berger. And Berger is hung up everywhere. As a prospective mother, I would just like to say that there is something highly unusual going on around here, and furthermore, Woof is hung up on Berger."

The next song, "Don't Put It Down," was the opening song at the Public, when it was called "Red, Blue, and White" and sung by Claude's parents. Here Berger, Woof, and a third tribe member have the honors, folding the flag with military precision but also using it briefly as a hammock for Woof. The tribe then rushes

THE TRIBE SHEILA FRANKLIN

By far the most passionately political member of the tribe, aka "Democracy's Daughter." Returns from a Washington, D.C. protest, where she helped "levitate" the Pentagon before being tear-gassed. Struggles to reconcile the members' professed idealism with their, at times, small-minded and selfish actions. Loves Berger.

James Rado has said Sheila is based in part on Janis Joplin, the hard-living, iron-throated rock singer (and noted *HAIR* fan,) and in part on Isabelle Blau, a devoted political activist who was in the Open Theater with Ragni and whose husband, Eric Blau, came close to producing *HAIR* in 1967. The Joplin influence can be heard somewhat in "Easy to Be Hard," the show's major ballad, but especially in more boisterous numbers like "I Believe in Love." Sheila's role has expanded over the decades: Tom O'Horgan reassigned "Easy to Be Hard" to her during Broadway rehearsals, and she would also assume one of Claude's speeches in later years.

into the audience to hand out flyers for the upcoming Be-In. As they leave (for one of the show's few costume changes), Jeanie gives Claude a book of instruction in astral projection. Only the waifish Crissy remains to sing "Frank Mills," about her hunt for a boy who lives somewhere in Brooklyn and has gold chains on his leather jacket. The song is similar in subject matter to "Donna" but could not be more different in tone.

The tribe reappears to the sound of tinkling bells; they are dressed in more decorative costumes and sing a minor-key version of "Hare Krishna." The Be-In has begun. The fire chalice also reappears, this time as a receptacle for the burning of draft cards. Several tribe members burn theirs before a conscience-stricken Claude briefly drops his into the flame, only to pull it out. Everything stops, and Claude's ambivalence about serving the country he loves bursts forth in the song "Where Do I Go?"

In counterpoint to Claude's musical plea, the tribe chants, "Beads, flowers, freedom, happiness." They disrobe and stand naked under dimmed lights. As the sound of police sirens begins faintly and quickly increases in volume, the stage lights go out and the tribe members run offstage carrying their clothes. It is then that two policemen announce that everyone in the audience is under arrest "for watching this lewd and obscene show." However, they quickly disclose that "it's only intermission."

ACT II

Hud brings a windup Victrola onto the stage, and Crissy puts on a record of Kate Smith singing "The White Cliffs of Dover." This morphs into the rock sound of "Electric Blues," sung by four tribe members dressed in the sort of reflective mirrors that would soon become associated with disco balls. Their psychedelic dance and light show, accentuated by several strobe lights and the flashlights that many cast members carry, is interrupted by a blackout. Berger reveals that Claude has disappeared and that he been looking for him for three days. Jeanie says she

ABOVE Gerome Ragni designed this Be-In flyer, which was passed out to audience members at the Biltmore.

BELOW LEFT The burning of the draft card from the 1968 production featuring Ragni, Rado, Curry.

BELOW The tourist "lady" reveals himself.

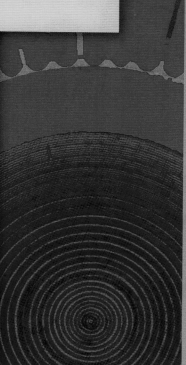

"I Believe in Love"

Sheila Franklin is introduced in all her activist glory.

JAMES RADO: *"It speaks for itself. 'I believe that now is the time for all good men to come to the aid of love.' Love needed some help, I suppose."*

I BELIEVE IN LOVE

I believe in love
I believe in love
I believe in love
I believe in love

I believe that now is the time
For all good men
To believe in love
I believe that now is the time
For all good men to come to the aid of...

My country tis of thee
Sweet land of liberty
God saaaaave...

I believe in love...

What do we want?
Peace
And when do we want it?
Now
What do we want?
Freedom
And when do we want it?
Now

Peace now freedom now
Peace now freedom now

(KKK)
What do we think is really great?
To bomb, lynch and segregate

(Tribe)
Black, white, yellow, red
Copulate in a king-size bed

Hey, hey, LBJ
How many kids did you kill today?

Hell, no, we won't go
Hell, no, we won't go

Peace now, freedom now

O GREAT GOD OF POWER

Oh great god of power
Oh great god of light
Oh great god of gas
Oh Con Ed, Oh Con Ed

Where has all the power fled?
Where has all the power fled?
He is blood
He is bone
He is air
He is

He is aquarius
He is aquarius

Appear, appear, appear

Manchester England England
Across the Atlantic Sea
And I'm a genius genius
I believe in God
And I believe that God
Believes in Claude
That's he

"O Great God of Power"

This chorale prays at the altar of the energy company Con Ed when the lights go out, conjuring Claude in the process. The cast carried candles in the darkness during this scene in 1968, and Lorrie Davis writes that an errant candle set Shelley Plimpton's hair on fire one night.

GALT MACDERMOT: *"That was written in previews. I'm not sure why they needed it, but it's quite nice. It's a charge."*

JAMES RADO: *"The blackout was a big thing in those days. That first one was a huge shock to our system—it was both exciting and disturbing."*

MICK JAGGER

The Rolling Stones' best-known and most acclaimed albums—*Exile on Main Street*, *Let It Bleed*, *Beggars Banquet*, *Sticky Fingers*—wouldn't come out until after *HAIR* debuted. But Mick Jagger had already emerged as a fully-fledged sex symbol with distinct androgynous appeal by the time Woof spoke of his long-standing and completely unrequited crush on the Rolling Stones frontman.

Jagger, as it happens, was long infatuated with American culture, particularly the blues. He and fellow Rolling Stone Keith Richards first met when Richards saw Jagger, then a student at the London School of Economics, carrying Chuck Berry and Muddy Waters albums on a bus. The Waters track "Rollin' Stone" provided the new band with its name, and four of its first five singles were covers of U.S. artists, including Buddy Holly and Willie Dixon.

From the beginning, Jagger's brash, strutting persona earned him the adoration of both men and women. The designer, photographer, and legendary esthete Cecil Beaton once described him as: "Mouth almost too large, but he is beautiful and ugly, feminine and masculine, a 'sport,' a rare phenomenon." Despite high-profile marriages to Bianca Pérez-Mora Macias and Jerry Hall (and children by two additional women,) rumors of Jagger's bisexuality have followed him for decades; as recently as 2008, Richards referred to "a load of excruciatingly painful campness" on his bandmate's part in a magazine interview. The most lingering piece of gossip came from David Bowie's ex-wife, Angela, who commemorated the end of the 10-year gag order that was part of her divorce arrangement by alleging on Joan Rivers's talk show that she had once caught the two men in bed together. Jagger and Bowie denied the allegation, and Angela Bowie subsequently backpedaled from the statement.

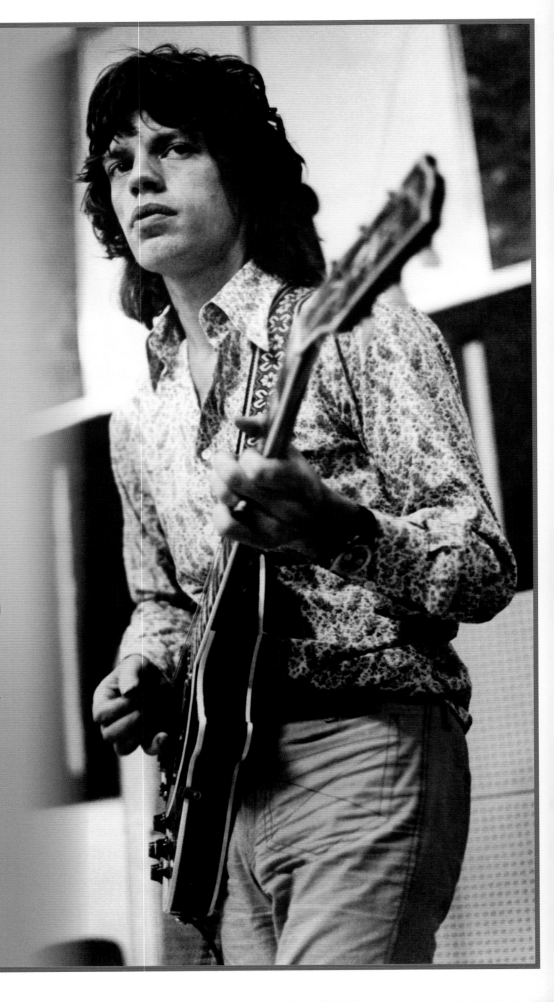

will conjure him, which leads into a candlelit ode to the energy company Con Edison, "O Great God of Power."

Her magic works, and Claude reappears in a gorilla suit driving a motorcycle through the orchestra and onto the stage. He describes his second visit to the induction center while Berger leads a dumb-show version of the draft board behind him. Claude then gives his prized possession, a Mick Jagger poster, to the extremely appreciative Woof.

One of the show's true showstoppers now takes place, as three of the tribe's white women sing to Hud about their attraction to him and the rest of the "Black Boys." Not about to be outdone, three of the black women (dressed in what turns out to be one massive piece of fabric) roll in on a 10-foot- (3-meter-) tall Plexiglas platform that slides toward the audience as they sing "White Boys" to Claude.

Hud turns out the lights, which come up gradually as first candles and then "glow worms" (marijuana cigarettes) are lit. First there is only the sound of inhaling, and then the tribe ties together universal consciousness, outer space, and psychedelic drugs in "Walking in Space."

Claude takes a hallucinogen and embarks on an epic psychedelic acid trip cum American history pageant that makes up much of the rest of the second act. It begins with a wigged Berger as George Washington ordering a bedraggled all-female troop to retreat, but not before four Indians slaughter the troop with bows and arrows. Ulysses Grant resurrects them, revealing a crazy quilt of American notables: three presidents (Calvin Coolidge, Teddy Roosevelt, and an elaborately dressed Abraham Lincoln,) one general (George Armstrong Custer,) one fictional character (Scarlett O'Hara,) and two actors (Clark Gable and John Wilkes Booth.)

This motley group dances a minuet before being attacked by three African witch doctors. Hud, the head witch doctor, berates Lincoln (who is being played by a black woman) on the country's history of racial inequity, culminating in the Vietnam War: "The draft is white people sending black people to make war on yellow people to defend the land they stole from the red people." They sing "Yes, I's Finished on Y'All's Farmlands." Lincoln responds with a spoken/sung version of the Gettysburg Address, complete with topical asides, as a white woman shines

Lincoln's shoes with her hair. The witch doctors become a Black Power trio and sing "Happy Birthday Abie Baby;" Booth shoots the birthday boy, but Lincoln pops up and says, "Shit, I ain't dying for no white man."

The attempted assassination kicks off a montage of death: Four Buddhist monks appear, one of whom is doused in gasoline and self-immolates in protest at the war. Three Catholic nuns strangle the remaining Buddhists with their rosary beads; they in turn are killed by three astronauts. The daisy chain of carnage continues as a succession of marauders (machine-gun-wielding Chinese, more American Indians, and finally Green Berets) each kills the preceding group, culminating with the Green Berets using their weapons on themselves. The stage is riddled with corpses, "ripped open by metal explosion," until a strobe light triggers a reversal. The bodies come back to life, leave the stage, and return for a speeded-up recapitulation, complete with the deafening sound of machine guns and other implements of war. When the sounds and strobe lights stop, the bodies are once more strewn across the stage, and everything is again silent.

As the sound of a bugle comes from the wings, a mother and father talk to a hanger holding an army jacket—a clear representation of their son. "Write me a letter," the mother says, and the father says how proud he is. A childlike melody plays in the background, and the bodies rise one by one in slow motion and begin playing children's games that degenerate into frantic, brutal war games.

The tribe sings "Three-Five-Zero-Zero," an adaptation of an antiwar Allen Ginsberg poem. Watching from above are two angelic young men who sing "What a Piece of Work Is Man," a soliloquy from *Hamlet*. But not even these two young men are safe from the "pestilent congregation of vapors" they have just described, and they join the bodies on the ground.

As the tribe awakens, they all join hands to sing a brief reprise of "Walking in Space." Claude comes down from his surreal trip and explains to Berger that all he wants "on this dirt" is to be invisible and to make miracles. "Blizzards," he commands, "come down in sheets, cover everything in beautiful white holy snow."

Sheila counters the prospect of Claude's departure with "Good Morning Starshine," a tender love song to the heavens. The tribe falls under its sway, joining her in a light-hearted dance. Crissy is carried to the stage from the audience on a mattress, and everyone sings about all the things that can be done in "The Bed." (This song was also cut from the 2009 revival.) The tribe members each wish Claude a good night to the strains of "Aquarius" and depart, leaving him alone on the bare stage. He sings "Ain't Got No" as he attempts to ward off an unseen but palpable threat; shots ring out and he disappears into the darkness.

The action moves to outside the army induction center on Whitehall Street, where the tribe has gathered for an antiwar protest at dawn: Berger and Hud bang maniacally on a metal washtub with drumsticks as Sheila leads the crowd in chanting "Hell, no! We won't go!" She and Berger go looking for Claude, who materializes in full uniform; in a realization of the ritualistic cutting of his hair in the prologue, he now has an army-issue haircut. He calls out to the tribe, but they cannot see or hear him.

The tribe freezes, and Claude sings "The Flesh Failures," followed by a brief reprise of "Manchester England." A trio sings in counterpoint "Eyes

INITIALS

LBJ took the IRT
Down to 4th Street USA
When he got there
What did he see?
The youth of America on LSD

LBJ IRT
USA LSD

LSD LBJ
FBI CIA

FBI CIA
LSD LBJ

"Initials"

This ditty pokes fun at the prevalence of three-letter sets of initials, positing a scenario where LBJ hops on the IRT to find today's youth on LSD.

GALT MACDERMOT: *"It's a song that has very little value. But everywhere you look these days, you see three initials. So maybe they were onto something."*

JAMES RADO: *"It's a little silly, but it's also a little daring to use the FBI and the CIA in the song, especially since the CIA had supposedly experimented with LSD."*

SELF-IMMOLATING MONKS

"No news picture in history has generated so much emotion around the world as that one," John F. Kennedy said. He was referring to Malcolm Browne's Pulitzer Prize-winning photo of Thich Quang Duc's self-immolation at a busy intersection in Saigon, South Vietnam, on June 11, 1963.

New York Times reporter David Halberstam was also present; he and the other U.S. correspondents had been informed the day before that "something important" would occur outside the Cambodian embassy in protest against the persecution of Buddhists by President Ngo Dinh Diem's Roman Catholic administration. Tensions between the Buddhists and Diem's government had been building for more than a month at that point, and many of the journalists skipped the event. Halberstam and Browne witnessed some 350 monks and nuns marching along with the blue sedan that held Thich Quang Duc and two other monks.

After emerging from the car, he sat in the traditional lotus position on a cushion in the road; the marchers then formed a circle around him to prevent the police (or well-wishing bystanders) from getting to him. A colleague poured a five-gallon gasoline can over Thich Quang Duc, who rotated a string of prayer beads and recited an homage to Amitabha Buddha before lighting a match. "His body was slowly withering and shriveling up, his head blackening and charring," wrote Halberstam, who also won a Pulitzer Prize for his reports. "In the air was the smell of burning human flesh; human beings burn surprisingly quickly."

The initial official response to the self-immolation was encouraging: An embattled Diem, whose regime was supported by the Kennedy administration, announced several reforms designed to relieve tensions. However, lingering disaffection and further protests led to a series of government raids on Buddhist pagodas in August of that year. (One such raid saw forces seize the intact charred heart of Thich Quang Duc, whose body had been re-cremated eight days after his death; the heart was deemed holy after surviving two incinerations.) This triggered several more self-immolations by Buddhist monks, and Diem was killed in an army coup that November. Many have pointed to Thich Quang Duc's suicide as the turning point of the six-month conflict.

Self-immolation soon became a potent form of protest toward the Vietnam War, and more than a half dozen Americans would ultimately commit the same act on American soil. As with Thich Quang Duc's death, many of these would take place outside buildings of power, including the Pentagon (below the office of Secretary of Defense Robert McNamara) and the United Nations Building. One such protester, a 56-year-old mother of two, burned herself to death in front of the Federal Building in Los Angeles. She died October 15, 1967—two days before *HAIR* premiered at the Public Theater.

Look Your Last," made up of other snippets from Shakespeare (culminating in "The rest is silence"). Claude moves away and is engulfed by the tribe. While they cannot see him, they clearly sense him and reach out to him. But he is gone, even to the audience.

Sheila and Dionne resume "The Flesh Failures," which leads into "Let the Sun Shine In" as the rest of the tribe joins them. They move together in a mournful throng, finally leaving Claude's corpse lying in the center of the stage. The only other person left on stage is Berger, who does a furious dance around Claude's body before dropping to one knee and raising his drumsticks above Claude's head in the shape of a cross. During a final refrain of "Let the Sun Shine In," the lights fade to black, until the only thing visible is Berger's makeshift cross, glowing in the dark.

But the rest is not silence. Not just yet, at least: The tribe reappears, and now it is the audience's turn to interact with the cast. The tribe swells to include however many audience members can flood onto the stage in time to join the cast in an exuberant final reprise of "Hair."

ABOVE LEFT Thich Quang Duc protests in 1963 in Saigon by setting himself on fire.

THE REVIEWS

The opinion of *The New York Times* had an even more profound impact on a Broadway show's success in 1968 than it does today, and although Clive Barnes had responded favorably to the Public production, the extent of changes meant his opinion of O'Horgan's production was still in question. And while Barnes had his reservations, particularly about some of the new songs, he christened it as "the first Broadway musical in some time to have the authentic voice of today rather than the day before yesterday."

A similar—and perhaps more portentous—statement came in an essay Barnes wrote four months later for the *Saturday Evening Post*. "The time has come for another revolution," he wrote, "and *HAIR* could be the musical to start it." Many theater professionals interpreted this and other similar statements from Barnes as a sign that the paper of record expected musicals to start adapting to a younger audience, and this may have been responsible for some of the animosity that *HAIR* generated among Broadway's old guard.

Barnes's enthusiasm for the show continued when he reviewed it a second time nine months after it opened and—to the amazement of some involved, who felt the onstage discipline and professionalism had dipped noticeably during that time—praised it again: "It still seems as though the whole thing is swiftly, deftly and dazzlingly being improvised before your very eyes." (Those naysayers within the company would agree with the "being improvised" part of that sentence, if not the "deftly" or "dazzlingly.") Barnes even went on to testify on the show's behalf during one of the legal tussles that would break out as *HAIR* moved beyond New York to less hospitable towns.

All this won him the unwavering support of Michael Butler. When most people think of the interactions between producers and critics, they probably think of Max Bialystock's attempt to slip the *Times* critic a $100 bill outside the theater in the film *The Producers* (which also debuted in 1968.) Butler's gift to Barnes was considerably more generous: a necklace with an authentic early twentieth-century buffalo-image nickel coin. "I never got a nickel necklace, nor did Joe," says Bernard Gersten, who, along with Joseph Papp, had anxiously watched Barnes nod off at the Public. "But Michael gave one to Clive."

(One of the blue notebooks that Michael Butler kept for bookkeeping purposes did in fact list Barnes, along with Harry Belafonte and Ellen Stewart, among the list of recipients, whom Butler referred to as "Silver Indians." "They were real buffalo nickels," he says, "and very expensive now. To get one, you had to be somebody who really did something for *HAIR* but who wasn't directly involved.")

As it happens, many of the Broadway reviewers shared some of Barnes's caveats and added a few of their own, but the overall tone was hugely enthusiastic. Words like "fresh," "daring," and "exciting" surfaced repeatedly. The only genuinely harsh

1968
THE YEAR OF

HAIR∞

The American Tribal-Love Rock Musical [I]

"BLOWS UP BROADWAY"
— Village Voice

"I FLIPPED"
— Klein, WNYC

"WONDERFULLY WILD"
— Jefferys, WABC-TV

"BOLD & OUTRAGEOUS"
— Watts, N.Y. Post

"SO LIKABLE, SO NEW, SO FRESH!"
— Clive Barnes, N.Y. Times

"HAIR," the American Tribal Love-Rock Musical, has exploded on Broadway — and Broadway is not likely ever to be the same again. Michael Butler is presenting this "musical be-in" which NBC's Leonard Probst hails as "the only new concept in musicals on Broadway in years and more fun than any other this season." In their outrageously funny book, Gerome Ragni and James Rado take a loving, living realistic look at today's flower children, with their bells, beads, incense, costumes, dreams and freaking out. A multi-talented cast that bristles with youth is turning everybody on with love and a whole new set of values.

Tom O'Horgan has pulled out all the stops in directing the frenetic fun set to the joyful rock music of Galt MacDermot. The Ragni-Rado lyrics shout *"I Got Life"* and *"I Believe In Love"* and sing the praises of *"Hair"* and *"White Boys"* and *"Black Boys"* and *"What A Piece Of Work Is Man."* Everything about **"HAIR"** is refreshingly free, uninhibited, honest and *now.* That's why 1968 is the year of **"HAIR."**

FOR INFORMATION, PHONE 265-4777

mainstream review came from the *Daily News*'s John Chapman, who called it "cheap, foul-mouthed, vulgar, and tasteless." Nearly every review mentioned (and often opened with) the nude scene, and the language and drug content also popped up in even the most favorable reviews.

Those who did criticize *HAIR* tended to do so on ideological grounds. William F. Buckley's review in the adamantly right-wing *National Review* rejected the show's messages as "pretty dreary, out of the poetry section of *The Worker*." He said, "Seeing *HAIR* makes one just a little prouder of middle-class establishmentarian standards."

However, the show also weathered its share of criticism from the opposite end of the political spectrum. The *Village Voice*, whose politics weren't as purely liberal as they are today (and whose apocryphal letter to the editor spawned "Frank Mills,") praised O'Horgan's innovations and the overall tone but described the roles of Claude and Berger as "unsympathetic and virtually unplayable." Perhaps the most scathing *HAIR* review, however, came from the *East Village Other,* arguably the house organ for the New York hippie scene. Citing student riots simultaneously unfolding at Columbia University, just a few miles away, the critic wrote dismissively of the "fun-loving tribal rockettes" being depicted at the Biltmore.

Still, these objections were more than outweighed by the overwhelmingly positive reviews by the likes of Barnes and John J. O'Connor of *The Wall Street Journal,* who predicted that the show would be "important to the history of the American musical." And *HAIR* received an additional boost from a relatively new medium: New York's television stations. Just as TV brought the Vietnam War to the public with an entirely new level of immediacy—directly into their living rooms, in (often bloody) color—the TV critics conveyed the sights and sounds of *HAIR*, which came into being largely as a counterweight to that war, even without the video clips that would ultimately become a central part of TV coverage.

Two particular blurbs found their way into as many advertisements as possible early in the run; both gave a clear signal of the notoriety that Michael Butler quickly realized would sell tickets. One came from Clive Barnes, who called it "the frankest show in town." The other blurb, from Allan Jefferys at New York's ABC affiliate, made a similar claim, only more floridly: "It makes *Marat/Sade* seem like *Peter Pan*."

ABOVE Claude is tarred and feathered early in *HAIR*. The show itself was largely spared a similar fate at the hands of the critics.

RIGHT An iconic image of Gerome Ragni.

LEFT Students clash during the Columbia University protests, which came to a violent close just hours after *HAIR* opened a few miles south.

THE PHENOMENON

"*HAIR* was marvelous for middle-aged people. They said, 'Oh, that's the reason my son is that way!'" That's how Joseph Papp described the appeal of *HAIR* to *Players Magazine* in 1970, and he raises a sound point. *HAIR* certainly attracted a younger, looser crowd than the typical Broadway fare of that (or any other) time. But even in 1968, when ticket prices went no higher than $11—although Michael Butler briefly flirted with selling $50 tickets to large corporations—the majority of the audience was of an age and tax bracket very different from that of the hippies in their midst. *HAIR* offered the older generation a fairly benign glimpse into the thoughts and actions of the hippie generation without sugarcoating it beyond what that generation would find palatable—never an easy combination. It served as a mirror but also a map.

This cross-generational appeal would result in a virtual parade of notables making their way backstage at the Biltmore. Walter Michael Harris, who at 16 was the youngest *HAIR* cast member, has fond memories of meeting Sidney Poitier, Janis Joplin, and even Salvador Dalí after performances. And Joplin didn't come alone: "I remember her and the rest of Big Brother and the Holding Company sitting in the front row and passing the jug up to the stage," Natalie Mosco says. James Rado has a fond memory of Carol Channing approaching Paul Jabara (who impersonated Channing at one point in the show) backstage and saying, "Mr. Jabara, I loved your impersonation of Bette Davis."

New York parties among a certain cosmopolitan set wouldn't be complete without a *HAIR* cast member in attendance. Their celebrity even trickled into ads for acne medication: A pair of television ads featured scantily clad tribe members "just at that age, draft age" singing the praises of Thera-Blem skin cream. (In an odd case of art imitating life, Shelley Plimpton and Ronnie Dyson would have cameo appearances in Robert Downey's 1969 spoof *Putney Swope*, where they touted the pimple remover Face-Off in a fake ad within the film.)

The print media also pounced on the show. There were the *Playboy* pictorials, yes, and a slightly less salacious article in *Esquire* grilling each female cast member about why she did or didn't participate in the nude scene. But there was also a major article in *Life* magazine (in an issue that featured "The Face of War" as the cover story) and a piece in *Ebony* that hailed *HAIR* as "the biggest outlet for black actors in the history of the American theater." Richard Avedon photographed Rado, Ragni, and Lynn Kellogg (the original Broadway Sheila) for *Vogue,* while Sally Eaton discussed her character's sign—"Aries with Cancer's problems"—for *Astrology Today*.

ABOVE Andy Warhol (center, with Rado and Ragni) was just one of many celebrities who came to see *HAIR*.

BELOW Ben Vereen (left,) who joined the Los Angeles cast of *HAIR* before joining the New York company, with the singer/songwriter/playwright/poet/civil rights activist Oscar Brown (right.)

RIGHT The sheet music for "Aquarius," one of several *HAIR* songs to yield numerous successful cover versions.

AQUARIUS

Words by JAMES RADO, GEROME RAGNI
Music by GALT MacDERMOT

FROM
THE MUSICAL
PRODUCTION

HAIR

THE AMERICAN TRIBAL LOVE-ROCK MUSICAL

LIFE I
VERY SHO

United Artists Music Co Inc.

UNITED ARTISTS MUSIC LTD.

Mortimer House, 37-41 Mortimer Street, London W1

Sole Selling Agents:Campbell, Connelly & Co. Ltd. 10 Denmark Street, London WC2H 8LU

20p

COLORED SPADE

I'm a
Colored spade
A nigra
A black nigger
A jungle bunny
Jigaboo coon
Pickaninny Mau Mau

Uncle Tom
Aunt Jemima
Little Black Sambo

Cotton pickin'
Swamp guinea
Junk man
Shoeshine boy

Elevator operator
Table cleaner at Horn & Hardart
Slave voodoo
Zombie
Ubangi lipped

Flat nose
Tap dancin'
Resident of Harlem

And president of
The United States of Love
President of
The United States of Love

(and for dinner at the White House
you're going to feed him:)

Watermelon
Hominy grits
And shortnin' bread
Alligator ribs
Some pig tails
Some black eyed peas
Some chitlins
Some collard greens

And if you don't watch out
The boogie man will get you
Boooooooooo!

Television continued to generate publicity, particularly through appearances on the major talk shows. Ed Sullivan, who got his start as a theater columnist, had long featured performances from current musicals on his program, but not many of these ended with the cast members engulfing the host with love beads and daisies. Rado and a barefoot Ragni chatted with a bemused Johnny Carson. Michael Butler and Elsie Dyson, the mother of 17-year-old cast member Ronnie Dyson, would occasionally join the cast on the different programs for renditions of "Let the Sunshine In" (the song performed most frequently, along with "Aquarius" and "Hair.") Tom Smothers spoke enthusiastically about the Los Angeles staging of *HAIR* on his show—failing to mention that he himself was producing it.

However, the biggest cultural impact of the show was felt on the radio and in the record stores. Until *HAIR*, rock music on Broadway had been relegated almost entirely to one-off songs in revues (as with the tellingly titled "I Don't Wanna Rock" in the 1957 edition of the *Ziegfeld Follies*, sung by a 50-year-old man playing a "Juvenile Delinquent.") The best-known musical before *HAIR*, 1960's *Bye Bye Birdie,* surrounds the pair of rock songs given to its Elvis Presley-esque character with an otherwise old-fashioned score. Suddenly, here was a score that was steeped in the harmonies, rhythms, and instrumentations of rock music from beginning to end, although Clive Barnes was astute to point out MacDermot's "strong soothing overtones of Broadway melody."

In a way that's unthinkable in today's climate, with theater playing a more marginal role and the notion of a unified "popular music" becoming a thing of the past, the *HAIR* cast recording became virtually inescapable. Rado

"Colored Spade"

Hud enters and spouts a series of racial epithets that culminate with the far more positive "President of the United States of Love." This and the prior two songs were discarded at the Public Theater.

GALT MACDERMOT: *"It was already written, but Freedman didn't want to do it."*

GERALD FREEDMAN: *"I wanted all those short songs out. You need breathing space so that the good numbers can really register."*

JAMES RADO: *"We thought these terrible words slammed all together made a point. And also, they look so wonderful together on the page."*

LORRIE DAVIS (PLAYED HUD A DOZEN OR SO TIMES DURING THE ORIGINAL BROADWAY RUN): *"One thing I made sure to convey was that this is not the way it is. This is what you call us, but this is not how it is."*

DARIUS NICHOLS (HUD IN 2009): *"The 'so you say' at the end [added in later versions] says it all. You may call us all these things, but that's not us."*

and Ragni had high hopes for their material—they complained to *Billboard* magazine in late 1968 that the subject matter of songs like "Black Boys" and "Colored Spade" had scared away recording artists—but not even they could have expected to see more than 700 recordings of *HAIR* songs by 1970. This would include chart-topping hits by The 5th Dimension ("Aquarius/Let the Sunshine In," which won a Grammy for Record of the Year,) the Cowsills ("Hair"), and Oliver ("Good Morning Starshine").

"There were about a dozen record shops on Broadway," Natalie Mosco says, "and every one of them would be playing *HAIR*. Diane Keaton and I would walk down Broadway, and you'd hear Three Dog Night singing 'Gliddy glup' and The 5th Dimension singing 'When the moon…' and it would go on and on. And we'd be like, 'Enough *HAIR*!'" This ubiquity reached a new level of oddness when Bob McGrath led a group of hippie Muppets in "Good Morning Starshine" during a 1969 episode of *Sesame Street*.

The "*HAIR*" album itself would spend 13 weeks as the top-selling recording in 1969. Its cover image—an adaptation of the Broadway poster, with Ruspoli-Rodriguez's mirror-image treatment of Steve Curry in acid green, yellow, and red, like an upside-down traffic light—became an iconic

ABOVE From left, Steve Curry, Steve Gillette and Lynn Kellogg.

LEFT Lamont Washington, the original Hud.

"Electric Blues"

A quartet kicks off the second act with this raucous cautionary tale about the encroaching age of electrification, with little more than "sonic armor" protecting everyone from "miles and miles of Medusan cord." Galt MacDermot used the song's main melody for the "Opening" that briefly served as an overture at the Public.

JAMES RADO: *"The arts were using video and all kinds of new media. Rock music had upped the decibels, and you had the feeling of how everything was escalating."*

GALT MACDERMOT: *"It's always been the beginning of the second act. Jerry hated electricity. He had sort of a hunch about stuff like that."*

ELECTRIC BLUES

Tell me who do you love man?
Tell me what man?
Tell me what's it you love man?

An old-fashioned melody

Tell me what's it that moves you?
Tell me what's it that grooves you?

An old-fashioned melody
But old songs leave you dead
We sell our souls for bread

We're all encased in sonic armor
Beltin' it out through chrome grenades
Miles and miles of medusan chord
The electronic sonic boom

It's what's happening baby
it's where it's at daddy

They chain ya and brainwash ya
When you least suspect it
They feed ya mass media
The age is electric

I got the electric blues
I got the electric blues

Thwump… rackety… whomp
Rock… folk rock… rhythm and blues
Electrons explodin'… rackety-clack
Thwump… rackety… whomp
Plugged in… turned on

We're all encased in sonic armor
Beltin' it out through chrome grenades
Miles and miles of medusan chord
The electronic sonic boom

It's what's happening baby
it's where it's at daddy

They chain ya and brainwash ya
When you least suspect it
They feed ya mass media
The age is electric

I got the electric blues
I got the electric blues

image of psychedelia, right down to the primitivist stencil creating a nimbus around his "shining, gleaming, steaming" hair.

The success of the *HAIR* recording led to something virtually unprecedented in the history of musical theater—an album devoted to MacDermot, Rado, and Ragni's discarded numbers. *DisinHAIRited*, which was released in late 1969, contained songs that hadn't fit on the original Broadway cast recording ("Going Down," "Electric Blues,") songs that were cut on the way to Broadway ("Exanaplanetooch," "The Climax,") and other bits of *HAIR* ephemera that never quite slotted into the show (including "I Dig," a musicalized version of Jeanie's monologue devoted to Claude's attributes).

Michael Butler and the show's publicist, Mrs. Michael Gifford, saw to it that *HAIR* never crept too far out of the limelight. "When I was in town, we would meet every morning and cook up ideas for keeping the Establishment freaked out," Butler says. One fairly innocuous (but expensive) way to publicize the show came through a series of lavish anniversary concerts during the four years it ran on Broadway. Three of these parties took place in Central Park, where as many as 15,000 attendees saw cast members joined by the likes of Shelley Winters and Oliver. The other birthday celebration took place in May 1971, when the action moved north to the Cathedral Church of St. John the Divine on 112th Street. There some 7,000 people watched Galt MacDermot lead the *HAIR* cast and the cathedral choir through a program that interspersed songs from the show with MacDermot's five-movement Mass in F.

ABOVE Tom Smothers (center,) who produced the Los Angeles production of *HAIR*, invited the cast on to his show, *The Smothers Brothers Comedy Hour*.

RIGHT Approximately 15,000 fans came to Central Park on May 7, 1972, to celebrate *HAIR's* fourth anniversary on Broadway.

GOOD MORNING STARSHINE

La da da da, da da da, da da da, da
da da da da
da da da, da da da, da da da da,
da da da da da

Good morning starshine
The earth says hello
You twinkle above us
We twinkle below

Good morning starshine
You lead us along
My love and me as we sing
Our early morning singing song

Gliddy glup gloopy
Nibby nabby noopy
La la la lo lo
Sabba sibby sabba

Nooby abba nabba
Lee lee lo lo

Tooby ooby walla
nooby abba nabba
Early morning singing song

Good mornin' starshine
The universe rings
With Milky Way music
Our blue planet sings

Good morning starshine
We're happy and strong
Sending you love from above
Our early morning singing song

Gliddy glup gloopy
Nibby nabby noopy
La la la lo lo
Sabba sibby sabba
Nooby abba nabba
Lee lee lo lo
Tooby ooby walla
Nooby abba nabba

Early morning singing song

(music interlude)

Can you hear us?

Singing a song
Loving a song

"Good Morning Starshine"

Sheila dispels the gloom of Claude's trip by leading the tribe in an "early morning singing song" on behalf of the twinkling earth.

JAMES RADO: *"The love for humanity emanates from the entire show. You know how when you love someone, you love the whole world? This expands it even further. You love the whole universe."*

GALT MACDERMOT: *"It's a singing song, a feel-good song. You need it at that point."*

HAIR HITS THE ROAD

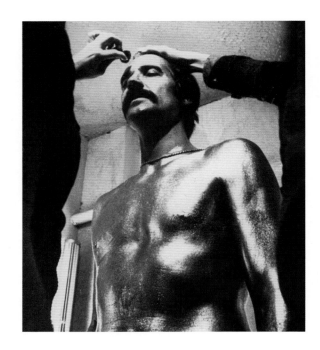

Like so many aspects of the Broadway business model, the protocol for expanding the reach of a successful show was and is fairly codified. If a show does well enough on Broadway to warrant a second company, that company—ideally with the original stars or, barring that, actors with some name recognition—either begins a tour or "sits down" in a large city (often Chicago or Los Angeles.) In the case of a very popular show, a second and maybe even a third touring and/or sit-down company will swing into gear.

Once again, Michael Butler's outsider status may have worked to his advantage. Butler approached the show with the zeal of a missionary—"I honestly believe *HAIR* is a message from God," he says—and missionaries aren't known for biding their time. By the summer of 1970, the tribe had expanded to include no fewer than 11 companies around the United States. In city after city, sit-down productions would morph into permanent bookings; the Los Angeles production, starring Rado and Ragni and featuring a handful of O'Horgan innovations that would make their way back to the New York production, would run for nearly 1,000 performances in the newly renovated and renamed Aquarius Theater. If it wasn't already, *HAIR* was now a full-fledged national phenomenon.

Each tribe was given its own name—the Chinook, the Wampanoags, the Chumash. And the touring companies' itineraries would be set in part by Maria Elise Crummere, Butler's astrologer, who had picked April 29 as a propitious opening night at the Biltmore. "We would have these bizarre itineraries on the basis of Maria's charts," says Bill Swiggard, who toured as Claude with the Mercury tribe. "We once went from Toronto to New Orleans and then to Ottawa." If Crummere suggested a 1,300-mile detour, Butler was inclined to take her suggestion. Not even the potential discomfort of opening the Tokyo production on December 7—the anniversary of the bombing of Pearl Harbor—got in the way of her choices.

As *HAIR* spread its message across the country with uncharacteristic speed, it met with pockets of resistance in cities both large (Boston) and small (Mobile, Alabama, where the cast and crew were escorted to the city limits by four police cars in the middle of the night). Harassment from local law-enforcement officials reached the point where Butler's office disseminated an eight-page handout titled *WHAT TO DO IF YOU ARE DETAINED, HARASSED, OR ARRESTED BY THE POLICE, SOME INFORMATION AND ADVICE.*

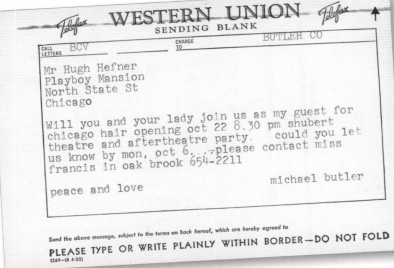

ABOVE A telegram from Butler inviting *Playboy* magazine founder Hugh Hefner to the opening night of *HAIR* in Chicago.

RIGHT Butler's office disseminated this eye-opening pamphlet to cast and crew members who were touring in less hospitable locations.

The following was written as general advice for the members of "Hair" and the staff and employees of Natoma Productions. Laws vary from state to state regarding various crimes and search and seizure. It is for that reason that this "advice" has been written mainly on the basis of Federal law, which, of course, supersedes state law.

Remember that this is designed as a guideline of what to do if you are arrested. Each situation is different as is each circumstance. If you are arrested and booked you should immediately contact your local "Hair" office which will in turn be able to refer you to an attorney who will give you further advice.

Above all else, don't panic and try to conduct yourself in a civilized manner. There are legal procedures which have to be followed once you are arrested and booked and there is nothing either you or the police can do about them.

Robert Fitzpatrick,
Attorney at Law
9000 Sunset Boulevard
Los Angeles, California 90069

WHAT TO DO IF YOU ARE DETAINED, HARRASSED
OR ARRESTED BY THE POLICE--SOME INFORMATION
AND ADVICE.

1. Show upon request your ID.

2. ASK if you are under arrest.

    a) If answer is no, then ASK why you are being detained.

    b) Then ASK if you are free to go.

    c) If the policeman states that you are under arrest--

3. ASK for what reason you are under arrest.

4. ASK to see arrest warrant.

5. Whether under arrest or not you have the following RIGHTS--

    a) the RIGHT to remain silent--take advantage of it and SHUT-UP.

    b) because anything you do say can be held against you.

    c) the RIGHT to see your attorney or to contact him.

6. If you, your car, or your abode is SEARCHED, ASK to see search warrant.

    a) If no search warrant, STRESS REPEATEDLY that you do NOT CONSENT to the search.

There are three different situations wherein the rights of the policemen as well as your own rights vary considerably. There is the street situation. There is the automobile situation. There is the house situation. In all three of these situation there is some of the time a considerable gap between the theory and the reality: what the police are permitted to do and what they actually end up doing are many times two different things. As true as it is for human nature, some policemen are good and some are bad. The bad policemen will act in total disregard of your rights: the end justifies the means. And most of them will enforce the law as they have been taught, and their subjective understanding of that law may be different from the way you know it.

THE STREET SITUATION

If the police confront you on the street and demand to see your ID, show it to them. You are required to produce your ID or be ousted if you cannot or will not.

The police have the right to protect their bodily safety--therefore if they reasonably believe that you are armed and dangerous, they can first frisk you, pat you down without going inside your pockets. If they discover something that feels like a weapon they then can go inside your pockets. If the policeman feels a hard metal bulge that might be a knife or gun he can search your person. However, he cannot go inside your pockets upon feeling a soft bulge, that of week or pills, on the pretext that he thought you were armed with a dangerous weapon.

The reality is that there are some policemen that are not so conscientious of your rights as others and with an overzealous desire to apply what they've learned of the law, they may see a different set of "facts", i.e., if they felt only a soft bulge, they'll more than likely search you anyway.

If instead of searching you the policeman asks you to empty your pockets, you ask WHY? If he answers because of a concealed weapon, ask him which pocket the weapon is located for you do not have any weapons on your person. Ask him to frisk you outside that pocket. If he grabs dope, look for witnesses. Pay attention to where you are located--residential neighborhood, tenement houses, business area etc. Look for open windows, passerbys, anybody to later testify as to what the police did.

Don't be a smart-ass. Let the police know that you are aware of your rights, but do it softly--save yourself a possible bump on the head for if they club you, they'll justify it by claiming that you, they'll justify it by claiming that you resisted arrest or assaulted a peace officer.

If you are drunk the situation is different again--they can arrest you and search you right on the spot.

You have the right to remain silent and to contact your attorney. Above all else, COOL IT and look for witnesses.

THE CAR SITUATION

A different set of rules apply here. The gap between theory and reality can be just as wide.

Make certain to keep your taillights and license plate lights in

---

working order. The policeman has the right to make a preventative detention of your car if you have an equipment violation. Also keep your traffic citations paid up. Whenever, your auto is stopped the police will check, as a matter of course, if there are any warrants out for your arrest. Carry your driver's license--if you do not have it with you, the police can arrest you on the spot, impound your car and later search it.

The police have the right to search your car if they have probable cause to believe that the car is being used in the commission of a felony, or if they believe that the car contains contraband. Probable cause to believe means that the belief must be a reasonable one, i.e., if a reasonable man under identical circumstances could believe that a felony probably is or was committed, then there exists the necessary probable cause for the police to search. Even if the police were mistaken and there was no felony, all that is required is that they reasonably believe that a felony occurred.

Some common situations that provide for probable or reasonable cause to search the auto are where the driver appears drunk, (or would so have appeared to the reasonable man acting under identical circumstances) or where the police smell alcohol or drugs. (If they smell alcohol and find drugs instead, they can still legally seize the drugs for they had sufficient probable cause in the first place to search when they smelled the alcohol.)

Do not make any furtive movements. The policemen will claim that they thought you were reaching for a weapon--they will search the car claiming that they feared for their safety. Stay in the car unless

---

instructed to get out. DO NOT CONSENT to the search. A common situation is where the policeman asks, "Do you have anything in this car that we should not see?" Of course you answer NO. Then he might follow with, "In that case you don't mind if we take a look!" BE EMPHATIC--Do not consent to the search.

THE HOUSE SITUATION

It is in this situation that the rights of the policeman have been more restricted. However, the gap between what the police are permitted to do and what they actually do can be just as wide.

There are three situations wherein the police can search your house: (1) with a legal search warrant, (2) without a search warrant but pursuant to a lawful arrest, (3) without a warrant but with your consent. If the police have an arrest and/or search warrant, they must first knock at your door, announce their purpose and demand admittance. If all of this occurs, then open up. However, there are two exceptions where the police do not need to knock but can simply bust your door in: if they believe that the person inside is armed and dangerous or if they fear that evidence will be destroyed.

The police can enter your house without a warrant if they have probable cause to believe that a felony has been or is being committed inside, and there is not sufficient time to get a warrant. Again, if in fact a felony was not committed, but the policemen reasonably but erroneously believed that a felony was committed, then their entry without a warrant will be upheld by the courts.

Normally the police must have a warrant to enter and search your house. Therefore, the first thing to do is to demand to see the warrant-- if they do not have one, object repeatedly to their entrance inside your house. Ask if you are under arrest. The police cannot search first, then arrest later. But if you consent to their search, then they need not arrest you first. So under all circumstances make sure to object to their search.

If they bust you in the front room, they can only search the front room. But they'll just as likely search the whole house anyway. Again locate your witnesses. You have the rights to remain silent, to see your attorney.

CONCLUSION

Some policemen feel that they are the sole repository of justice. Thus to some the end invariably justifies the means. If that particular policeman is the type to just as soon beat you on the head as listen to your peaceful protest, then the best advice is to shut-up and do not resist. BE COOL.

BE COOL.

The glut of companies also gave Butler some latitude in terms of casting. Outstanding touring or sit-down performers would often find themselves rotated into the Broadway company; by contrast, Broadway performers could be dropped into a touring show fairly quickly if need be. The Washington, D.C. company, which included several once and future members of the Broadway cast, became known as Superstar *HAIR*.

This flexibility would be used to curious effect as *HAIR* began to proliferate internationally. Natalie Mosco went to Paris to choreograph that city's production and ended up learning to speak French phonetically so that she could play Jeanie, a role she later repeated in Melbourne. A similar thing happened by necessity when *HAIR* expanded into regions with small African-American populations; several black actors from the West Coast companies were flown to Japan, where they learned the roles of Hud, Dionne, and the other black characters phonetically.

With very few exceptions, the international rollout of *HAIR* went smoothly. This involved a bit of patience in England: The Lord Chamberlain, whose role of licensor of plays made him the country's de facto censor, had refused to license the play in the summer of 1968. And so the producers bided their time until the British Parliament passed a bill in October abolishing the office's censorship capability; the day after the bill became law, *HAIR* opened at the Shaftesbury

BELOW Leaflets advertising a special Independence Day performance (far left) and the final performance in Washington, D.C.

ABOVE A rehearsal of *HAIR* at London's Shaftesbury Theatre in 1968.

RIGHT Paul Nicholas and the rest of the London cast rehearse on September 25, 1968—one day before the British Parliament passed a bill paving the way for its opening.

ABOVE The West End cast rehearses.

LEFT Princess Margaret meets some of the cast members at a charity show at the London Palladium on December 8, 1968.

Theatre to 15 minutes of cheering—and several shouts of "Rubbish!" from the balcony. Rado and Ragni co-directed the Toronto production in 1970, joined by choreographer Julie Arenal, and the two men were sufficiently pleased with the talent and the energy they encountered there that they put the song "So Sing the Children on the Avenue," which had been cut off-Broadway, back into the show.

The international production that excited the writers most was arguably *Kosa*, the name given to the show in Belgrade, Yugoslavia, where it opened soon after the short-lived easing of Communist restrictions in Eastern Europe in 1968. Complete with comedic digs at Albania and Mao Zedong but devoid of references to draft dodging, this drastically revised production (the first *HAIR* to be directed by a woman) was a huge success. The management was forced to board up the theater's skylight out of concern for the hundreds of people climbing to the roof to see it for free. Marshal Tito, the president of Yugoslavia, was said to have enjoyed the show, but apparently not enough to leap onstage to join the cast in the title song, as Rado and Ragni did.

Bertrand Castelli, Butler's executive producer, was particularly instrumental in cultivating these productions and adapting them to the local circumstances; he made the then highly unusual decision of having the cast of each country perform *HAIR* in their own language. Later on, Isabelle Blau (the model in part for the character Sheila Franklin) became the international production coordinator, operating a sort of global quality control as she traveled the world and oversaw the various productions.

Occasionally, one country or another would prove resistant to the show's charms. Rado and Ragni came to regret their decision to attend opening night in Acapulco, Mexico—which also turned out to be closing night. The police padlocked the theater that night and arrested the cast and crew, many of whom had come from the Los Angeles company, before ordering them to leave the country; Rado and Ragni, who had hidden under a bed during the roundup, would ultimately join the rest of the company in hiding in a mountain resort for three days. (Nina Machlin Dayton, the *HAIR* archivist, points out that this production as well as one in Italy, also notably unsuccessful, were the only ones not suggested by Maria Elise Crummere.)

Other less consequential flashpoints included Bergen, Norway, where the outraged local population tried to create a human barricade to block the performance; Montreux, Switzerland, where the Protestant ministry made a similar, more formalized attempt; and Buenos Aires, Argentina, where approval was given only after a Catholic priest had attended a preview.

The Munich, Germany production was also contentious at first: One hotel turned away Rado and Ragni, and the two later ended up at a police station after a cab driver refused to take Ragni as a fare. The Culture Ministry threatened to shut down the production unless the nude scene was cut; after a spokesman for the show replied that his relatives had been marched into Auschwitz in the nude, Castelli had the tribe cover itself during the Be-In with a banner bearing the names of Auschwitz and other concentration camps. The nude scene was reinstated for the rest of the run.

Perhaps the most surprising international mounting of *HAIR* was a tour of U.S. bases in Vietnam, made up in part of members of the Philippines company. While Castelli was (understandably) prevented from offering

ABOVE Earl Scott, the Broadway company's official tarot card reader.

TOP The Be-In leaflet from the London production.

ABOVE Auditions for the Munich, Germany, production. Donna Summer, whom Bertrand Castelli had already hired, is second from left.

RIGHT The poster used to advertise *HAIR* in Munich.

LEFT Rehearsals for the Munich production.

RIGHT The cast of *HAIR* cavorts with two policemen on the streets of Munich.

BELOW When the German Culture Ministry protested the nude scene, Castelli responded with this pointed jab at recent German history.

soldiers a full production, the cast did perform the songs in a concert format, and Castelli said at the time that the response was quite favorable.

Another unexpected production took place closer to home, at Memphis State University, now known as the University of Memphis. A 1970 ABC News special called "When *HAIR* Came to Memphis" (which went on to win an Emmy Award) shows an intrepid college professor named Keith Kennedy running a gauntlet of initially concerned administrators and coaxing a 37-member cast, which included two Vietnam veterans, through the first nonprofessional production of the show—minus the nude scene. The students' struggles to reconcile their fundamentalist Christian beliefs with the show's messages are stirring, as are the sometimes charged interactions between the white and black cast members. (MSU had only begun admitting black students a decade earlier.) The cast would later perform the songs to some 250,000 audience members at the Atlanta Pop Festival, and Kennedy would later direct a production of the little-performed Ragni/MacDermot musical *Dude* in Florida.

HAIR

Ce n'est pas une pièce de théâtre normale
Ce n'est pas une comédie musicale normale
Ce ne sont pas des acteurs normaux
Ce n'est pas un metteur en scène normal
Ce n'est pas un adaptateur normal
Ce n'est pas non plus une soirée normale
Mais n'allez pas en conclure que c'est une histoire de fous, c'est une histoire de sage.
Ce soir, vous allez prendre un coup de drogue, un coup de soleil, un coup d'amour, un coup de folie. Certes, vous n'allez pas, aussitôt vu, aussitôt entendu et compris, vous laisser pousser les cheveux et vous mettre à chanter : " Je n'ai pas d'argent, je n'ai pas de boulot, je n'ai pas 20 ans, je n'ai pas de pot " mais j'ai : " une tignasse qui s'élève dans le vent comme un grand cerf-volant".
En vous, à l'intérieur et autour de vous, HAIR va cheminer, HAIR va pousser des pointes, HAIR va établir des têtes de ponts, HAIR va faire des comparaisons, HAIR va donner une nouvelle dimension, HAIR va viser et tirer sur la longue, longue cohorte de fantômes qui quotidiennement vous étranglent, HAIR va assassiner les démons et les tabous, HAIR va vous faire rêver debout, HAIR va vous remettre debout. Voir HAIR, c'est voir Clair.

JACQUES LANZMANN

TOP LEFT The end of the final peformance of *HAIR* in Hamburg, Germany, in 1970.

BOTTOM LEFT The same cast outside Hamburg's town hall.

ABOVE This essay was included in the French program for *HAIR*.

RIGHT Castelli gives the Paris company instructions during rehearsals in 1969.

ABOVE Julien Clerc as Claude leads the Paris cast.

RIGHT James Rado and Gerome Ragni had a particular soft spot for the Belgrade, Yugoslavia, production.

OUTRAGE AT HOME

Popular culture made a fairly rare appearance on the cover of *Time* magazine in the week of April 26, 1968. In a mixture of scandalized and respectful prose, the cover story hailed the young talent behind a shocking new work that had occasioned "heavy breathing on all sides." This work was not for the squeamish, it warned: "The sexual scenes, and the language that accompanies them, are remarkably explicit, even for this new age of total freedom of expression." The article's synopsis covered the protagonists' interminglings all the way to "the desperate tribal rites that come to consume [their] lives."

The subject was the new John Updike novel *Couples,* which dealt with sex far more explicitly than *HAIR* ever had or ever would. (*Time's* mixed-to-negative review of the musical ran two weeks later, dismissing the nude scene as "such a dimly lit still life that it will leave most playgoers open-mouthed with yawns.") Nonetheless, both in New York and (especially) as it began its rapid spread across the country, *HAIR* became a lightning rod of controversy. The nude scene played a major, but by no means the only, role in the furor that would see *HAIR* reach the U.S. Supreme Court twice in the next seven years—including one case that began in Boston, just 30 miles away from the fictional town of Tarbox, Massachusetts, where Updike situated his own desperate tribal rites.

It was in Boston that Garrett Byrne, a district attorney, saw the show in previews and attempted to prevent opening night—scheduled for February 20, 1970—from ever happening. After a court hearing, one in which *New York Times* critic Clive Barnes came to Boston to testify on the show's behalf, the Massachusetts State Supreme Court said the show was protected under the First Amendment if it clothed the actors "to a reasonable extent" during the Be-In scene and excised "all simulation of sexual intercourse or deviation." The producers refused to make these changes, and rather than risk arrest for the entire cast, the Boston production shut down on April 10.

For the next six weeks, Butler kept the idle Boston cast and crew on full salary while the case made its way through the courts, armed with letters of support from Actors' Equity and numerous other organizations. A three-judge panel at the U.S. District Court of Boston issued a new injunction on May 6 that shielded the cast from prosecution; the Massachusetts authorities obtained a temporary stay of the injunction. On May 22, the Supreme Court decided not to extend that temporary stay by a 4–4 vote, saying that the forced changes would have "a chilling effect on the right of free expression." *HAIR* opened at the Wilbur Theatre the next day, with no changes to the text or staging.

(The decision involved only eight justices because Harry Blackmun, who was appointed by Richard Nixon, had been confirmed by the Senate just 10 days earlier and had not yet been seated when the case was argued. Thurgood Marshall, one of the more liberal justices and a consistent supporter of individual

ABOVE Supreme Court Justice Thurgood Marshall, seen here at the funeral of Martin Luther King Jr., would cast a crucial vote in favor of *HAIR* in 1970.

RIGHT Mira Trailovic, the director of the Belgrade, Yugoslavia, production, sent Julie Arenal this telegram while the Boston production sat in limbo.

NNNN

ZCZC CLB0227 RMD1837 YJU237

URCL CO YUBE 047

BEOGRAD/3 47 14 1915 AM

File
Boston Hair

JULIE ARENAL

HAIROFFICE 236 WEST 55 STREET NEWYORK N Y

WE MOURN WITH YOU THE SUPPERETION OF HAIR IN BOSTON MASSACHUSETS
STOP WE HOPE SOME DAY BOSTON WILL ENJOY THE FREEDOM OF ARTISTIC
EXPRESSION WE JOY IN BELGRADE PRODUCTION OF HAIR
LOVE AND PEACE MIRA TRAILOVIC BELGRADE HAIR COMPANY

COL 236 55 STREET

LEFT Although the staging of "Don't Put It Down" had become less contentious by the time *HAIR* returned to Broadway in 2009, the scene was extremely controversial in 1968.

RIGHT *Apollo 13* astronauts Fred Haise, James Lovell, and John Swigert with President Nixon the day after their safe return on April 17, 1970. Lovell and Swigert would soon generate headlines by walking out of a performance of *HAIR*.

BELOW The *Apollo 13* Lunar Module, also known as "Aquarius," acted as a lifeboat for the three men when an oxygen tank exploded onboard the *Apollo 13* Service Module.

rights, was ill at the time but voted in favor of the production from a hospital bed in Bethesda, Maryland.)

Unlike with the Boston production, which began previews but was temporarily forbidden to officially open, *HAIR* didn't even make it to the first preview in Chattanooga, Tennessee, before the authorities issued a restraining order in 1972 that would hold for almost three years. Once again, the ruling finally reached the U.S. Supreme Court; once again, *HAIR* was victorious. This time, however, the ruling did not address the contents of the show. Rather, it ruled that the refusal of access to the city's civic auditorium amounted to "unlawful prior restraint" on the part of Chattanooga's theater board. "A free society prefers to punish the few who abuse rights of speech after they break the law," Blackmun wrote in his majority opinion, "rather than to throttle them and all others beforehand."

Not every *HAIR*-related protest made it to the courts. Some were confined to the theater lobby, where an angry clergyman released more than a dozen white mice in St. Paul, Minnesota. Others took place inside the theater itself, and the main source of outrage appeared to be not the nudity or the drugs or the profanity but the perceived disrespect shown toward the U.S. flag. Furious audience members confronted the actors during "Don't Put It Down" on more than one occasion, and two U.S. astronauts reportedly stormed out of the theater at the same point.

Upon further investigation, however, the latter case proved to be a slight exaggeration. James Lovell and John Swigert, who made up two-thirds of the fabled *Apollo 13* mission, did attend a performance at the Biltmore in June 1970. "We didn't know exactly what it was when we went in," Lovell says. "In our minds, the show was sacrilegious. We had just come back from the mission, and the way they treated the flag didn't sit right with us. So as soon as the intermission came, Swigert and I and my wife left the theater. I mean, everyone left the theater to smoke—we just didn't come back."

Despite his reservations about the staging, however, Lovell was sympathetic to the show's antiwar message. "They were right on about that, and the music itself is terrific—I quite liked 'The Age of Aquarius [sic].'" As it happens, "Aquarius" was also the name of the lunar module that kept the three *Apollo 13* astronauts alive.

The indignation would occasionally—and, in one possible instance, tragically—spill into threatened or actual violence. Bomb threats were issued in several cities, including several times when a touring company reached Cleveland, Ohio, in the spring of 1971. A few weeks into the run, a fire in the hotel where the *HAIR* company was staying resulted in seven deaths, including the wives and young daughters of cast member Jonathan Johnson and production stage manager Rusty Carlson. Johnson's daughter was just two weeks shy of her first birthday. The cause of the fire has never been determined, and Johnson is one of several company members who believe the notoriety of *HAIR* had a lot to do with why the police never opened an arson investigation, despite the threats beforehand and the detonation of an actual bomb at the Hanna Theater in Cleveland shortly thereafter, which resulted in dozens of broken windows but no injuries.

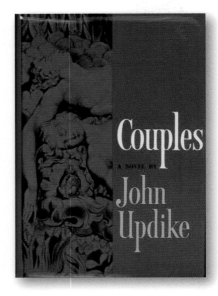

ABOVE With its considerably more explicit sexual content, John Updike's novel *Couples* also generated controversy in the spring of 1968.

RIGHT One of the many voices of protest lodged in response to *HAIR* and its perceived unpatriotic message over the years.

February 23, 1970

Manager
Wilbur Theatre
252 Tremont Street
Boston, Massachusetts

Dear Sir:

My understanding from the Boston Herald Traveler is
that your theatre is presently housing a "musical" that
manges in some way to abuse the American flag.

As a patrictic American with a responsibility to provide
leadership to many thousands of war veterans who fought
under this flag, I must sharply object to its abuse. I
am asking veterans not only to abstain from attendance
at this production but to join me in protesting this
current display of vicious un-Americanism.

Those who hate America should leave it. Purveyors of
pornography, filth and nudity will always find a willing
market. Those who desecrate a flag, however, should be
prosecuted.

It is my sincere hope that Hair will have an early and
permanent closing.

Yours sincerely,

John H Harold

John H. Harold
AMVETS State Commander

JHH/emd

TONY AWARDS

While the skirmishes around an awards show can hardly compare with free-speech cases at the Supreme Court, Michael Butler found himself fighting on behalf of *HAIR* within the New York theater community as well as on the national front. From the beginning, he had met with a chilly reception from the League of American Theaters and Producers, which had complete jurisdiction over the Tony Awards.

HAIR was originally denied consideration because it had begun previews after the eligibility cutoff date; Butler sued on the grounds that the date had been moved back from April 3 to March 19, despite his receiving assurances months earlier of the later date. "They changed the dates so that we could not qualify for the Tonys," Butler says today. Next came a determination that the show's origins off-Broadway invalidated it for contention. (Nearly a third of the Best Musical nominees of the last decade, including such winners as *Spring Awakening* and *Avenue Q,* would have been invalid according to this rule.) Butler even offered to produce a fully staged one-night-only performance on March 19 for the sole purpose of making the earlier deadline; this, too, was rejected.

By the time *HAIR* was finally allowed to compete, the 1968 Tony Awards had come and gone. Indeed, enough time had elapsed by the time the 1969 Tonys were given out that one original cast member was nominated for the performance she gave *after* leaving *HAIR*—Diane Keaton, for *Play It Again, Sam.* Keaton lost, which put her in good company with her former *HAIR* costars.

(Keaton, who refuses to be interviewed about *HAIR,* was among the first cast members to leave the show. Natalie Mosco remembers seeing Keaton talking with former classmates from the Neighborhood Playhouse, where she had studied, after the *HAIR* cast had attended a performance of the dark British comedy *A Day in the Death of Joe Egg.* Mosco says she was "bemoaning the fact that they were doing Chekhov and Shakespeare while she was stuck in *HAIR.*")

The musical competition was far stiffer in 1969: The fellow nominees for Best Musical that year included *Promises Promises*, which also drew heavily from pop-music idioms, and the Revolutionary War–themed *1776.* By contrast, the 1968 nominees included such little-remembered efforts as *Illya Darling* and *How Now, Dow Jones*; none of the four nominees lasted an entire year on Broadway, and that year's winning musical, *Hallelujah, Baby!* (which had briefly been advertised with James Rado as the male star), had closed more than three months before the ceremony.

With the exception of a heartfelt introduction by Harry Belafonte, who hailed "the impassioned plea of today's young people" before the current cast gave an abridged rendition of "Three-Five-Zero-Zero/What a Piece of Work Is Man/Let the Sun Shine In," the overall tone at the awards ceremony was one of barely concealed derision. In just the first few minutes, Carol Burnett could hardly keep

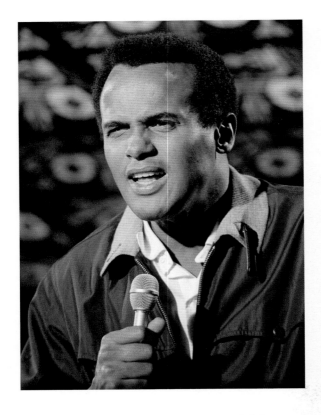

ABOVE Harry Belafonte; singer, actor, social activisit, and one of the few people at the 1969 Tony Awards to be supportive of *HAIR*.

RIGHT Zero Mostel with Gene Wilder in the 1968 film *The Producers.* Mostel mocked *HAIR* during the Tony Awards.

RIGHT Diane Keaton with Woody Allen in the film *Play it Again, Sam* (1972.) Keaton was nominated for a Tony Award in 1969 for her performance in the stage version of this, rather than for her role in *HAIR*.

LEFT Ethel Merman in 1964 celebrating being booked to star in *The Talk of the Town*. Merman presented the 1969 Tony Award for Best Musical award to *1776*, a category which *HAIR* was also nominated in.

from stifling a snicker in listing *HAIR* among the year's contenders. (This tone was hardly limited to what happened on camera: Lorrie Davis writes of doing O'Horgan's sensory exercises on the floor with the rest of the cast during the Tony rehearsal only to see Shelley Winters getting down onto the ground with them and mimicking their actions.)

Rado's and O'Horgan's names were mispronounced by Zero Mostel and Ethel Merman, respectively, and Mostel began his Best Musical presentation by stating, "I thought *HAIR* was extraordinary, didn't you? [Not insignificant applause.] But I must tell you, it reminds me of my son's room. [Considerably heartier laughter.] They just left my house!" Mostel then gave the Best Musical award to *1776*, which had already won in the other category for which *HAIR* was nominated, Best Direction of a Musical.

In today's culture, where anything smacking even mildly of pomposity is punctured almost instantly, such scoffs are commonplace. But the general tone was far more sincere 40 years ago, and the scorn directed toward *HAIR*—which, it should be remembered, had been running for more than a year at this point and contributing heavily to the economic health of Broadway—is indicative of the mistrust and worse that dogged the show even within these presumably more collegial circles.

HAIR FATIGUE

Lorrie Davis, who played Abe Lincoln and one of the three "White Boys" singers, is the only member of the original Broadway cast to publish a memoir of her experiences. *Letting Down* My *HAIR* created a mild furor when it was published in 1973, and many of the parties involved have accused Davis of misrepresenting them and/or their actions. But the book serves as a potent record of the curdled idealism and dissipating morale that affected much of the cast. "As *Hair* grew, it fell apart," she wrote.

This decline is notable not because of where the mood ended up—the vast majority of *HAIR* alumni have overwhelmingly positive memories of their time in the show—as much as where it began. From the beginning, when Tom O'Horgan lobbied to have the cast actually live in the Biltmore, a gauzy utopianism rested over *HAIR* and its message. As long as the tribe took seriously its commitment to love, peace, and equality, the rest would take care of itself.

Like every other utopian scheme before or since, this scenario was inherently doomed. "People compete, and they get jealous, and they nurse grudges," says Julie Arenal. "It's human nature, and there's no reason why this group would be any different just because they're singing about peace."

The conflict was by no means confined to the Broadway company. Robert Camuto, who played Claude and Woof on several tours, remembers standing in a hotel parking lot in Norfolk, Virginia, and talking to a curious theatergoer who was asking if the company was as harmonious and loving in real life as it appeared to be on stage. Camuto assured the man that it was—just as two of the female cast members fell to the ground in a fistfight a few feet away.

LEFT Donna Summer (seen at center, singing "White Boys") was one of many notables to join the *HAIR* cast over the course of its lengthy run.

ABOVE Gerome Ragni and James Rado would periodically return to the company—and not always on the best of terms.

RIGHT The original cast performs "Hashish."

"Hashish"

In the first of several short songs, the cast rattles off a litany of mind-altering substances, from the ancient (peyote) to the pharmaceuticals that were proliferating at the time (LSD, Dexedrine.)

GALT MACDERMOT: *"When Jerry and Jim were writing the show, they saw a band who had a lot of introduction songs. And they wanted to do a lot of these sort of short songs for the opening. Jerry didn't like dialogue."*

JAMES RADO: *"I'm not sure which band Galt would be referring to. I guess either the Fugs or Frank Zappa. Probably the Fugs."*

HASHISH

Hashish
Cocaine
Opium
Marijane
LSD
DMT
BMT
A&P, IRT
APC, alcohol
cigarettes, shoe polish, cough syrup,
peyote
Equanol, dexamyl, composine,
chemadrine,
Thorazine, trilofon, dexadrine,
benzedrine, methedrine,
S-E-X Y-O-U WOW!

JULY 1970   FROM MICHAEL GIFFORD

HAIR - FACT SHEET

~~AS OF JANUARY 1, 1970~~ OVER ~~5,350,000~~ *10,000,000* PEOPLE AROUND THE WORLD HAD SEEN HAIR. AUDIENCES HAVE INCLUDED EVERYONE FROM PRINCESS ANNE (WHO HAS SEEN HAIR TWICE) TO PRINCE MIKASA, BROTHER OF THE EMPEROR OF JAPAN, WHO TERMED THE SHOW "VERY PHILOSOPHICAL".

726 RECORDINGS HAVE BEEN MADE FROM THE SCORE IN THE UNITED STATES, GERMANY, ENGLAND, ITALY, HOLLAND, SPAIN, SWEDEN, ARGENTINA AND FRANCE BY SUCH ARTISTS AS NINA SIMONE, BARBRA STREISAND, DIZZY GILLESPIE, THE SUPREMES, LESTER LANIN, MANTOVANI, PETER NERO, PERCY FAITH, ETC.

OVER ~~2,500,000~~ *5,000,000* ORIGINAL CAST ALBUMS CONTAINING THE COMPLETE SCORE HAVE BEEN SOLD ~~IN THE UNITED STATES.~~ *WORLDWIDE*

HAIR COMPANIES HAVE PERFORMED THE MUSIC FROM THE SHOW ON EVERY NATIONAL TELEVISION SHOW INCLUDING MERV GRIFFIN, THE TONIGHT SHOW, ED SULLIVAN, ETC.

HAIR WAS THE FEATURED PRODUCTION ON LAST YEAR'S TONY AWARDS.

HAIR IS PLAYING TO FULL HOUSES IN NEW YORK, LOS ANGELES, SAN FRANCISCO, CHICAGO, LAS VEGAS, SEATTLE, TORONTO, BOSTON, DETROIT, PARIS, LONDON, SAO PAOLO, GERMANY, HELSINKI, BELGRADE, SYDNEY AND *TEL AVIV ROME FRANKFURT, MONTREAL, MIAMI*

-2-

AMSTERDAM, AND PLAYED LIMITED RUN ENGAGEMENTS TO AUDIENCE AND CRITICAL ACCLAIM IN TOKYO, STOCKHOLM AND COPENHAGEN.

IN THE UNITED STATES HAIR EMPLOYS OVER 300 MEMBERS OF ACTORS EQUITY AND 200 MEMBERS OF I.A.T.S.E.

FAMED COLUMNIST LEONARD LYONS COMMENTED LAST YEAR FOLLOWING THE PULITZER PRIZE AWARDS, "IF THE PULITZER PRIZE COMMITTEE AND EXERCISED ANY GUTS OR INTEGRITY THEY WOULD HAVE VOTED FOR HAIR".

WHAT DOES THE WORLD THINK OF HAIR?

"IF YOU HAVE JUST ONE SHOW TO SEE ON Broadway...MAKE IT THIS ONE!"
                                        Clive Barnes, NY Times

"MAGNIFICENT IN ITS INFECTIOUS FRENZY...LOVE, LOVE, LOVE"
                                        John Du Pre, The People, London

"YOU LEAVE POSITIVELY GLOWING...THE LIVELIEST BASH IN TOWN...!"
                                        Dan Sullivan, L.A. Times

"BEST MUSICAL OF THE B'WAY SEASON"   Leonard Harris, CBS-TV

"THIS EVENING OF THEATER ENDS AT THE BARRICADES--THE BARRICADES PAVED WITH LOVE"
                                        Le Monde, Paris

"A MASSIVE, SPONTANEOUS, ALL EMBRACING TOUR DE FORCE...MAGNIFICENT"
                                        The Australian, Sydney

***

50,000 MILES OF "HAIR"

(The History of a Show Business Phenomenon
Arriving _____ at the _____ Theatre.)

It had been so long since even one song from a Broadway musical hit the very top of the country's best-seller charts, that few people thought it would ever happen again.

Then, suddenly, an American tribal-love rock musical called HAIR was all over the nation's airwaves. It's original cast album was No. 1, destined to become the biggest seller of all time, and four of its songs, "Aquarius," "Let the Sunshine In," "Hair" and "Good Morning Starshine" were gracing the Top 10.

HAIR was on its way to becoming an international institution, with new companies springing up in the United States and throughout the world. But it didn't quite begin that way.

It was back in the early part of 1967 that two disreputable-looking characters named Gerome Ragni and James Rado walked into the office of music expert Nat Shapiro, carrying a withered briefcase filled with notes and drawings on brown paper bags, napkins and old

envelopes, which, when pieced together, turned out to be the first draft for the lyrics and script of HAIR. They and their work were dedicated to the non-philosophy of non-violence, love, exploration of the senses and a demonstrative rejection of materialism. Their first concern was finding a suitable composer.

Shapiro, inspired to say the least by their creative effort, introduced them to Galt MacDermot, a square-looking Staten Island resident with four children, who somehow understood and loved the kind of music they were seeking. Within 36 hours he had completed six songs and come up with a thousand ideas. Within four days the show had been completed and was ready for a producer.

HAIR began making the rounds, but no one knew what to do with a free-style, 25-character folk-rock-oriented musical about a tribe of lovable kids who smoke pot, burn their draft cards and trade their chicks. Jerome Robbins, with whom Ragni had been studying and working, loved it, but was too busy. A few other producers and directors were intrigued but unconvinced that it could be commercially practical. Some were offended by its four-letter words and others by its violent put-down of the establishment.

Then along came Joseph Papp, who chose HAIR as the vehicle to launch his partially subsidized New York Shakespeare Festival at the downtown Public Theatre. It opened for a limited

eight-week engagement and was an immediate sell-out, but it soon had no where to go.

Michael Butler, a young, attractive, energetic, resourceful Chicago millionaire, was turned on by the show and then fell hopelessly in love. He was determined to keep it alive.

HAIR was moved lock, stock and props to Cheetah, a mid-town discotheque, which, it developed, was in a building about to be torn down. It looked like HAIR would again be cut off in its prime.

Butler then took over completely, buying the rights from Papp, allowing the authors to revise the work without any restriction, and bringing in Tom O'Horgan to enlarge the show's scope and give it a new dimension. The work was begun and on April 29, 1968, HAIR was firmly transplanted at the Biltmore Theatre on Broadway.

That the night would prove historic was something no one at that time could predict. But the reviews quickly confirmed that HAIR was indeed a milestone in the American musical theatre and that Broadway would never quite again be the same.

Since then, HAIR has indeed become an international institution. It is on its way to breaking every known box office record in New York, Los Angeles, Chicago and San Francisco, while continuing to flourish in London, Paris, Sydney, Duesseldorf,

Berlin, Munich, Tel Aviv, Toronto, Amsterdam, Copenhagen, Sao Paolo and even behind the Iron Curtain in Belgrade. Yearly grosses are topping $23,400,000, making it the most successful production in the history of the stage. New productions keep springing up around the world and several film companies have already bid over $2,000,000 for the movie rights.

The end is no where in sight. The main reason for its greatness, however, is that it is one of a kind. There can never be another HAIR.

*****

LEFT The official *HAIR* press kit from 1970.

ABOVE Ronnie Dyson, Donnie Burks, and Lamont Washington. Washington's death in August 1968 led to considerable tension within the tribe.

Attendance became an issue: Davis described one Christmas performance where two of the five leads and an additional five chorus members were all no-shows. Danny Sullivan, who was hired as an assistant stage manager after *HAIR* had opened—and who would later become better known as the Tony Award-winning director Daniel Sullivan (*The Heidi Chronicles, Proof*)—says Michael Butler entrusted him with "sort of taking care of the show." This would often involve playing the dramaturgical equivalent of an air-traffic controller.

"Who showed up was a big problem," Sullivan says. "Even though everyone technically covered everyone, you had to have pretty deep knowledge of who could do what—and who would be OK politically, in terms of who Jim and Jerry got along with and who had seniority over who."

Sometimes no-shows would be preferable to the antics that would occur on the stage: upstaging other actors, improvising beyond the established parameters, general bad behavior backstage. The typical cast member could be handled if need be; Emmeretta Marks, Jonathan Kramer, and other longtime cast members were fired and rehired at least once, and Paul Jabara was once fired mid-show. All of these comings and goings led to their own complications. Sullivan remembers seeing James Rado, who had ostensibly left the show by this time, and Steve Gamet, Rado's replacement, both sitting on stage preparing to play Claude one night. "I knew—I don't know how—that Jim didn't like the idea of Steve doing it," Sullivan says, "but I figured, 'What the hell, it's only for one night.'" Sullivan had to come out on stage—with his headset on—and cajole Gamet into leaving the stage before the opening vamp of "Aquarius" could begin.

When Rado and Ragni returned to New York from the Los Angeles production in the spring of 1969 brimming with new ideas, it wasn't long before Michael Butler himself had to step in. The two of them, along with two other actors, had already been ejected from the Aquarius Theater in L.A. after they walked up the aisle naked during the nude scene.

"Jerry got totally out of hand and was running up and down the orchestra with a red feather up his ass," says Butler, who periodically received *HAIR*-related complaints from no less than New York's mayor, John Lindsay. "And Jimmy would just follow Jerry around." Rado defends the aforementioned use of the feather as "an old bit of stage business" and points out that Ragni had often stuck one between his buttocks during "Sodomy" for a laugh.

Management, fearing a police raid, terminated Rado's and Ragni's contracts for "deviating from the standard performance in violation of the Equity production contract," and for about a week, the two were barred from the theater. They, in turn, filed charges with the Dramatists Guild, maintaining that they had a right to at least attend rehearsals in their capacity as co-authors. Galt MacDermot was brought in to intervene, as was Ellen Stewart of La MaMa. Butler first suggested that he, Rado, and Ragni air out their differences at the home of his friend Peter Yarrow (of the folk trio Peter, Paul, and Mary), but the summit eventually took place at the Sheep Meadow in Central Park instead.

Long after the two had officially left the show, visits were not unheard of, especially by Ragni. "Jerry would just walk in from time to time and announce that he was going on," says Merle Frimark, who began working in the *HAIR* publicity office in 1970. "The Equity rules went out the window," she says, referring to the stage actors' union that monitors cast replacements.

But the biggest wedges—the two things that threatened to poison the tribe's existence irreparably—were not absenteeism or the occasional bit of misbehavior or even a fistfight in a hotel parking lot. They were race and drugs.

On the one hand, the black community was largely heartened by the integrated nature of the tribe: *Ebony* magazine called the show "unquestionably the biggest outlet for black actors in the history of the American theater." And for the most part, neither the potentially incendiary subject matter nor the inherent discomfort of having black men speak racial epithets written by white men caused much trouble. Several cast members, however, say a fissure briefly appeared during rehearsals on April 4, 1968, when cast member Ronnie Dyson ran in announcing that the Rev. Martin Luther King had been shot. "Suddenly," Davis wrote in *Letting Down My HAIR*, "an invisible wall went up dividing the cast right down the middle: black vs. white."

The tension largely dissipated after a few days. But while several other race-related events registered on the national consciousness over the next six months—riots in several U.S. cities in the wake of the assassination, the black power salute offered by two medal-winning runners at that year's Olympic Games, shootouts between militant black groups and police in Cleveland and Oakland—it took a far more personal incident to threaten the stability of the *HAIR* company.

Less than four months after *HAIR* opened, Davis went to a rock club in Midtown Manhattan on a night off with Lamont Washington, who played Hud, and another cast member. Washington invited them back to his apartment on West 15th Street, but they declined. Davis got a frantic phone call a few hours later from Washington's manager, who told her that Washington had been badly hurt in an apartment fire; Washington, who jumped from his second-floor window onto the roof of an adjacent one-story building, would spend the next 15 days in St. Vincent's Hospital with burns over at least 50 percent of his body before dying on August 25 at the age of 24. The funeral service was scheduled for the following Wednesday morning, and Davis and Ronnie Dyson suggested to Fred Reinglas, the production stage manager, that that day's matinee be canceled.

Washington was not the most popular cast mate, and a handful of performers felt it would be hypocritical to attend the funeral of someone about whom they felt so ambivalent. Still, most of the cast went. When they began returning to the theater just a few minutes before the beginning of the matinee (which had not been canceled), several of the black cast members said they were unable to perform. The situation escalated until Davis and Michael Butler had a loud argument on the street, and the result was a matinee performed entirely by the white cast members. The part of Hud was split up among Rado and several other actors, some of whom held scripts.

"Freddy Reinglas coerced me into playing Abe Lincoln," says Natalie Mosco, who typically played the tribe member who shines Lincoln's shoes with her hair. "And what a bad idea that was. It was horrible." (Her compromise was to change the line "Shit, I ain't dying for no white man" after the assassination attempt to "I'm not dying—I'm only the understudy.")

Some resentment lingered among the black performers toward their white counterparts, but their anger was directed more toward the producers who

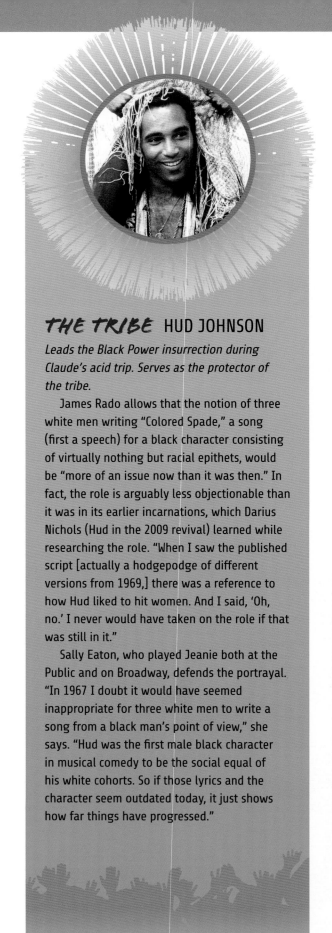

THE TRIBE HUD JOHNSON

Leads the Black Power insurrection during Claude's acid trip. Serves as the protector of the tribe.

James Rado allows that the notion of three white men writing "Colored Spade," a song (first a speech) for a black character consisting of virtually nothing but racial epithets, would be "more of an issue now than it was then." In fact, the role is arguably less objectionable than it was in its earlier incarnations, which Darius Nichols (Hud in the 2009 revival) learned while researching the role. "When I saw the published script [actually a hodgepodge of different versions from 1969,] there was a reference to how Hud liked to hit women. And I said, 'Oh, no.' I never would have taken on the role if that was still in it."

Sally Eaton, who played Jeanie both at the Public and on Broadway, defends the portrayal. "In 1967 I doubt it would have seemed inappropriate for three white men to write a song from a black man's point of view," she says. "Hud was the first male black character in musical comedy to be the social equal of his white cohorts. So if those lyrics and the character seem outdated today, it just shows how far things have progressed."

"Four Score/Abie Baby"

Abe Lincoln (played by a black woman) riffs on the Gettysburg Address to a doo-wop background. The quartet then wishes "Abie Baby" a happy birthday before John Wilkes Booth ends the celebration—or at least tries to. In *Letting Down My HAIR*, Lorrie Davis describes how she evolved her one line in the script ("Present, sir") into the jive-talking Gettysburg Address with the encouragement of first Gerome Ragni and then Tom O'Horgan.

GALT MACDERMOT: *"That was more of a rap than a song. Jerry asked me to write a melody for the movie of HAIR, but they didn't end up using it." [This new version has since been incorporated into the score.]*

JAMES RADO: *"She [Davis] thinks she introduced it, but she didn't. We were involved in the kind of theater where a lot of people tried a lot of different things, but then we went back and wrote it."*

ABIE BABY

Yes, I's finished on y'alls farmlands with yo' boll weevils and all
pluckin' y'all's chickens, fryin' mother's oats in grease. I's
free now, thanks to yo', Massa Lincoln, emancipator of the slave
Yeah, yeah, yeah, emanci-mother-fuckin-pator of the slave

Four score
I said four score and seven years ago
Oh sock it to 'em baby, you're sounding better all the time!
Our forefathers, I mean all our forefathers
Brought forth upon this here continent a new nation
Concieved, conceived like we all was
In liberty, and dedicated to the one I love
I mean dedicated to the proposition
That all men, honey, I tell you all women
Are created equal

Happy birthday, Abie baby
Happy birthday to you
Happy birthday, Abie baby
Happy birthday to you
Bang!
Bang? Ha ha. Bang, my ass! I ain't dying for no white man
(Tell it like it is, Leroy)

FAR LEFT Ron Williams as Hud in the Munich, Germany, production.

LEFT Saycon Sengbloh performs "Abie Baby" in the 2009 Broadway revival.

BELOW Even after the enthusiasm for *HAIR* dwindled, the spirit of protest remained.

refused to cancel the performance. "From that point on," Davis wrote, "the feelings of the tribe—the trust, togetherness, comfort, contentment, even respect—were badly shaken." That evening's performance marked the first time that a "black power" sign appeared on stage during the finale.

A similar sense of indignation surrounded what was perceived as a double standard in relation to two national tragedies: Davis writes how management replaced the typical post-show dance party with a moment of silence after the Kent State shootings in May 1970 but made no similar effort when three black students were killed 10 days later at Jackson State University. (The moment of silence was added for the following performance at Davis's request.)

All the while, the substances that the cast extolled and sometimes ingested on stage were taking their toll in real life. The hippies differentiated in theory between what are loosely defined as "head drugs" and "body drugs." Mind-expanding drugs like pot and LSD were good; depressants like opiates and alcohol were bad.

Rado says he and Ragni, who actively disliked pot, did several performances while on mescaline "The colors were intense," he says. Original cast member Robert I. Rubinsky has similar memories of dropping acid at the beginning of the show one night. Rubinsky remembers making eye contact with a fellow cast member who had also taken acid and thinking "Whoa."

Still, pot was by far the most common drug: Several cast members say the marijuana cigarettes being smoked on stage in Act II were not always props. Frimark remembers bringing her schnauzer to the theater on matinee days. "He would run up the stairs to where the dressing rooms were and get a contact high."

"My Conviction"

A tourist lady (actually a man in drag) gives an anthropological explanation of how long hair on guys actually represents a sort of evolution "into the gaudy plumage which is the birthright of his sex."

GALT MACDERMOT: *"That was a real speech that [the anthropologist] Margaret Mead wrote. I mean, that's what they told me."*

JAMES RADO: *"Yes, that's a Margaret Mead quote. Modified slightly, but that's her."*

TOP LEFT This eerie photograph depicts original cast members Steve Curry, Paul Jabara, Lamont Washington, Natalie Mosco, and Ronnie Dyson on a cast trip to a Long Island beach.

LEFT Shelley Plimpton would play Crissy on Broadway until 1972.

In reality, though, the substances taken didn't divide quite so neatly between "good" and "bad." The most troubling manifestation of this came from the official company physician, Dr. John Bishop, at whose office the cast sang Sally Eaton's baby into the world. Bishop, who had previously served as Timothy Leary's physician, offered the cast free (at first) weekly shots to keep their energy up. He called them Vitamin B-12 shots, but it is an article of faith among nearly all of the remaining cast members that they were in fact laced with amphetamines. "We were told that this Dr. Bishop was coming in to give us vitamin shots," Lipari says. "For some reason, he picked me as the first recipient. I go up, he gives me the shot, and I start to faint. What he had in that needle overwhelmed me. And he said, 'Oh, there must have been a little bit too much for her.'"

Once the dosages were worked out, the shots became a weekly ritual for much of the cast. "You'd do half the shot before the matinee and then bring the second half back to the theater," Natalie Mosco says.

"You tasted the Vitamin B-12 mode in your mouth instantly," Lipari says, "and then you felt the speed mode. And when you crashed, you got a bit of depression. So after about three tries, I was done with that."

While some cast members downplay the effect of these injections—"I don't think Dr. Bishop's shots were the downfall of *HAIR*, " says Walter Michael Harris— others are convinced that these were at least partially responsible for the drug addictions that would afflict so many of them. (At least two original cast members died from drug-related incidents, and many others grappled with addiction.)

Michael Butler, who had hired Dr. Bishop as the company physician, scoffs at such accusations. "I wouldn't be surprised if there was something in the shots beyond the vitamins," he says, "and it doesn't concern me one iota if there was. I don't know if we could have opened when we did had Dr. Bishop not given those shots—there was so much flu and other illnesses among the cast at that point."

In Act I of *HAIR*, one of the faux tourists makes a fervent speech defending the rights of today's youth to experiment, to push the boundaries. "Kids," she says, "be free, no guilt, be whoever you are, do whatever you want to do, just as long as you don't hurt anyone." Several of the original cast members were still in their teens when *HAIR* opened, and too many of them lost sight of the fact that doing whatever they wanted—whether under the advice of the company physician or on their own—could amount to doing harm to themselves.

"It takes discipline and constant effort to keep a show tight eight times a week, week after week," Harris says. "That's true about any Broadway show, but one thing that I think worked against *HAIR* was the sort of loose, improvised nature." The very things that made the *HAIR* cast so unusual— their youth and verve and spontaneity—made them perhaps less well suited to maintaining that discipline.

Tom O'Horgan, the man more responsible than any for creating this level of institutionalized anarchy, came to realize the toll this protracted level of intensity would take on such unseasoned performers. "Any professional actor would only give a certain amount of himself to a performance, knowing how to space himself over that period," O'Horgan is quoted as saying in *Letting Down My HAIR*. "This is something we intentionally didn't want to have, and in doing so we were asking for trouble.

"No one can give the kind of stuff the kids in *HAIR* do and hold up. You just can't."

THE MIDDLE YEARS

In the wake of *HAIR* and its success, it was inevitable that other musicals would try to replicate its sound and vibe. Most of these were unsuccessful; Galt MacDermot alone had two rock musicals flop within the space of six weeks, *Dude* (cowritten with Gerome Ragni) and *Via Galactica*. However, a handful of other shows managed to harness the rock sound that Broadway had first begrudgingly and soon covetously accepted as a way to reach younger audiences. James Rado (along with his brother, Ted) had a small-scale success with *Rainbow*, an unofficial sequel to *HAIR* that opened off-Broadway in late 1972. Tom O'Horgan applied his unconventional methods to the Andrew Lloyd Webber/Tim Rice musical *Jesus Christ Superstar* in 1971, casting such *HAIR* alumni as Ben Vereen and Ted Neeley. *Grease* followed a similar trajectory to *HAIR*, transferring from off-Broadway in 1972; *Godspell* also made the jump, although not until after five successful years off-Broadway. Still another transfer, 1971's *Two Gentlemen of Verona*, with a book by John Guare, reunited MacDermot with the Public Theater.

While none of these shows had the cultural impact or barn-burning success of their 1968 forebear, they combined to gradually sap *HAIR* of its must-see status. In addition, the two cultural milestones most closely linked with the show had each begun to lose their currency by 1972: The Vietnam War had entered its protracted endgame, with only 641 U.S. casualties that year compared with more than 16,500 in 1968, and nudity had lost much of its shock value through far more explicit glimpses of flesh on stage (*Oh! Calcutta!*) and screen (*Midnight Cowboy*, the only X-rated film to win an Oscar for Best Picture.) By the time the hardcore pornographic film *Deep Throat* began attracting the likes of Johnny Carson and Truman Capote to theaters in June 1972, a few dimly lit seconds of stationary hippies hardly seemed scandalous.

Michael Butler believes that his mission to spread the show around the country as quickly as possible also affected business on Broadway. "*HAIR* was young people talking to older people," he says, "and we couldn't wait to carry that discussion wider. And I have no doubt that the New York run was curtailed as a result."

On May 17, 1972, more than four years after it opened, *HAIR* first posted a closing notice for later that week. Word of its imminent departure spurred a brief flurry of sales, and the show lingered for another six weeks. When it finally closed, on July 1, it had logged 1,750 performances, making it the 10th-longest-running show in Broadway history at the time. (Numerous shows have since surpassed this number.)

The national touring companies continued for a little more than a year, at which point *HAIR* began its lucrative second life under what are known as secondary rights. The licensing agency Tams-Witmark was entrusted to

ABOVE James Rado and Gerome Ragni made a surprising cameo as policemen in the 1977 Broadway revival of *HAIR*.

TOP RIGHT Dorsey Wright, Annie Golden (who also appeared in the 1977 revival,) Treat Williams (as Berger,) and Don Darcus in the 1979 film of *HAIR*.

BOTTOM RIGHT Jeanie (Sally Eaton) emerges from her bomb shelter to sing "Air."

"Air"

After a peace chant morphs into an expanded version of "Ain't Got No," Jeanie appears to sing this tongue-in-cheek tribute to air pollution, which ends in a fit of coughing.

GALT MACDERMOT: *"Every day Jerry and Jim would read the paper and say, 'We gotta do a song about this.' And I think they saw something about the environment."*

SALLY EATON (CREATED THE ROLE OF JEANIE): *"At first I wasn't crazy about 'Air,' or being called the Sulfur Dioxide Girl! But it was a great honor to perform 'Air' at the first Earth Day and many other Green events. 'Air's range isn't much of a challenge for a vocalist—I can sing it today as well as ever. The song has truly stood the test of time, so maybe 'Air' and I have a future."*

AIR

Welcome, sulfur dioxide!
Hello, carbon monoxide!
The air, the air
Is everywhere

Breathe deep while you sleep
Breath deep

Bless you, alcohol bloodstream
Save me, nicotine lung steam

Incense, incense
Is in the air
Breathe deep while you sleep
Breathe deep

Cataclysmic ectoplasm
Fallout atomic orgasm
Vapor and fume
At the stone of my tomb
Breathing like a sullen perfume
Eating at the stone of my tomb

Welcome, sulfur dioxide!
Hello, carbon monoxide!
The air, the air
Is everywhere

Breathe deep while you sleep
Breathe deep! (Cough)

Deep! (Cough)

Deep, da-deep! (cough cough)

LEFT, RIGHT AND BELOW
Michael Bogdanov directed a revival of *HAIR*, starring John Barrowman and Paul Hipp, at London's Old Vic Theatre in 1993.

BELOW RIGHT The London 1993 "White Boys" trio was made up of Sinitta, Pepsi Demacque, and Felice Arera.

authorize productions by everything from professional regional theaters to high schools.

Unlike other titles of the time, which modified their content for more easily offended communities (*Grease* being the most obvious example,) *HAIR* never scaled back the drug references, the language, or even the nude scene to make it more palatable. "If you're uncomfortable with the show, you're probably not going to do it in the first place," says Sargent Aborn, the president of Tams-Witmark. "And if you sanitize it, it's really not *HAIR* anymore."

Butler was eager to reintroduce the show to New York audiences, however, and he made the surprising decision to bring *HAIR* back to the Biltmore, once again directed by O'Horgan, in 1977—just five years after the original had closed. Revivals have become far more common on Broadway than they were at the time, but even by today's standards, five years is an extremely quick turnaround. Michael Butler had once again bucked the typical way of doing business on Broadway. This time, however, the gamble failed: Critics pounced on the show, situating it in an awkward middle ground of being too old to be relevant and too new to work as a period piece, and it shut down after just 43 performances.

Looking back, MacDermot, Rado, and Butler all feel the timing was wrong for a revival. "The world didn't want any part of *HAIR* at that point," MacDermot says. And Butler and Rado both expressed misgivings about the casting. "The whole business of living as a tribe—that was a key part of every production I've done except the 1977 production," Butler says. "It was assembled as a commercial production, with casting people and so forth."

LEFT A scene from
the original Austrian
production of *HAIR*.

ABOVE The poster for the
2002 production of *HAIR*
in Vienna.

RIGHT A 2003 revival
of *HAIR* in Sydney,
Australia (bottom) saw
the cast members sing
for peace on the steps of
Sydney Town Hall (top.)

All the while, the drumbeat of a film version—which had been discussed practically since opening night in 1968—had grown steadily louder. Butler says Hal Ashby (*Shampoo*) and Luchino Visconti (*The Leopard*) were among those discussed as possible directors, and Butler had coveted Colin Higgins, who was best known at the time for writing the screenplay for *Harold and Maude*. But the assignment finally went to Milos Forman, who had approached Rado and Ragni after a performance at the Public back in 1967 and requested a copy of the script. Forman, whose films in his native Czechoslovakia had already earned him a reputation among cineastes, tried to interest Czech producers in mounting a stage production in the Communist country, but to no avail.

It wasn't until 1975, when Forman's *One Flew Over the Cuckoo's Nest* became an Oscar-winning smash success, that he was considered a viable candidate from a financial point of view. Rado says he and Ragni were excited about having Forman direct, but the relationship soured when Forman declined to use a film treatment that the two co-creators had written; instead, he used an entirely new screenplay by the young writer Michael Weller, who had made an impressive debut with the similarly themed 1971 play *Moonchildren*.

Forman proved to be a shrewd judge of talent: Weller and the film's choreographer, Twyla Tharp, each went on to considerable success, as did all three of his lead actors, Treat Williams, John Savage, and Beverly D'Angelo. But Weller's screenplay completely transformed the narrative

from a free-form immersion into the hippie subculture into a fish-out-of-water drama with an elaborate plot. Claude (Savage) became a straitlaced rancher who stumbles on a Central Park Be-In on his way to the induction ceremony; Sheila (D'Angelo) transformed from a gritty NYU undergrad to a Long Island debutante; and Berger (Williams,) Ragni once complained, was more of "a madcap village idiot" than a ringleader. The New York-specific setting gave way to a sprawling tale that stopped down in Oklahoma and Nevada (filming took nearly a year,) with "Good Morning Starshine" accompanying a cross-country road trip and a last-minute prank resulting in Berger, not Claude, flying off to his death in Vietnam.

The movie, remembered now as an out-of-touch curiosity, had its proponents at the time. Vincent Canby of *The New York Times* called it "a rollicking musical memoir" with "the charm of a fable and the slickness of Broadway show biz at its breathless best," and the $13 million it earned at the box office was respectable if by no means earthshaking. (*Grease*, which followed in *HAIR*'s footsteps on Broadway, beat it to the big screen by nine months; it would become one of the most successful films of all time.) Still, most of the creative team—even MacDermot, who reorchestrated his score for the film—say Forman's *HAIR* bears next to no resemblance to the stage version. Rado believes the definitive *HAIR* movie has yet to be made.

As time went on, productions in places like Sarajevo, Bosnia (formerly Yugoslavia) demonstrated the show's continuing appeal to young people in revolt everywhere. Meanwhile, modern-day parodies on "The Simpsons" and *The 40-Year-Old Virgin* (which punctuated the title character's climactic deflowering with a full-cast rendition of "Aquarius/Let the Sunshine In")

ABOVE Sharon Lawrence, Megan Mullally, Karla DeVito, and John Mahoney perform songs from *HAIR* for charity at the Alzheimer's Association 11th Annual "Night at Sardi's" in 2003, a celebrity-heavy revue and awards show.

LEFT Dorian Harewood at the Sardi's event.

RIGHT The original cast (with the notable exception of Lorrie Davis) joins hands for the show's finale.

LEFT A 2004 production of *HAIR* in France.

THE FLESH FAILURES / LET THE SUN SHINE IN

We starve—look
At one another
Short of breath
Walking proudly in our winter coats
Wearing smells from laboratories
Facing a dying nation
Of moving paper fantasy
Listening for the new told lies
With supreme visions of lonely tunes

Somewhere
Inside something there is a rush of
Greatness
Who knows what stands in front of
Our lives
I fashion my future on films in space
Silence
Tells me secretly
Everything
Everything

Manchester England England
Manchester England England
Eyes look your last
Across the Atlantic Sea
Arms take your last
Embrace
And I'm a genius genius
And lips oh you the
Doors of breath
I believe in God
Seal with a righteous kiss
And I believe that God believes in Claude
Seal with a righteous kiss
That's me, that's me, that's me
The rest is silence
The rest is silence
The rest is silence

Singing
Our space songs on a spider web sitar
Life is around you and in you
Answer for Timothy Leary, dearie

Let the sunshine
Let the sunshine in
The sunshine in
Let the sunshine
Let the sunshine in
The sunshine in
Let the sunshine
Let the sunshine in
The sun shine in...

"Flesh Failures/Eyes Look Your Last/Let the Sun Shine In"

Shakespeare makes a second appearance in "Eyes Look Your Last," as the tribe sings a passage from *Romeo and Juliet* while first Claude and then other tribe members sing modern, abstract lyrics. ("Listening for new told lies / With supreme visions of lonely tunes.") Unexpectedly, almost imperceptibly, the song morphs into "Let the Sun Shine In," which is not so much an invitation as a plea.

GALT MACDERMOT: *"That first part was originally designed to be read as a poem in front of the Waverly in Act I. Jerry really couldn't be bothered listening to words unless they were set to music. If you read that lyric, it's a somber lyric. When I got to the chorus, I had to repeat 'Let the Sun Shine' to fill out the line."*

JAMES RADO: *"['Flesh Failures'] was always a mysterious lyric to me—it was to many people. It's a kind of free verse, which Galt gave a real form. And then suddenly the simplicity of 'Let the Sunshine In' literally lets light in."*

have embedded *HAIR* more and more deeply as a pop-cultural touchstone, a title familiar to people born years or even decades after the Summer of Love.

Even as *HAIR* in its standard form became a perennial among college and other nonprofessional groups, a handful of productions took a more ambitious approach. Rado has spoken with dismay about a Copenhagen production in the late 1990s, which jettisoned the original script and used the movie screenplay, and a subsequent production in Vienna, in which Claude opened the show by having a tattoo burned into him.

In 2005, a more welcome rethinking came in London when a 26-year-old American named Daniel Kramer updated the text (with Rado and MacDermot's permission) to include references to September 11, the Kyoto Protocol, and George W. Bush. And years before Baz Luhrmann reached global fame as a film director with brazen works like *Moulin Rouge!* and *Strictly Ballroom*, he interpolated much of the text into the stage production *Haircut*, in which a group of 1980s club kids take a mind-altering substance and suddenly find themselves in *HAIR*; Natalie Mosco, who lived in Australia for 20 years, replicated the original staging.

The highest-profile mounting of *HAIR* during this time came on May 26, 1988, with a decidedly unconventional twentieth-anniversary benefit concert—chaired by Nancy Reagan, no less—at the General Assembly Hall of the United Nations. Original cast members were reunited from around the world, and the casts of two college productions served as the tribe. Barbara Walters served as host for the black-tie affair, which had a top ticket price of $5,000 and included nine new songs from *Sun*, a new piece that Rado and Ragni were writing at the time. Bea Arthur (whose rendition of "Black Boys" included a racy new stanza that Rado wrote for the occasion,) Dr. Ruth Westheimer, and Donna Summer were just a few of the 163 performers who took part. This concert, by many accounts, made up in energy what it lacked in polish. Walter Michael Harris recalls a brief midsong interaction with Ragni. "Somehow, in the middle of this train wreck, Jerry and I caught each other's eye and we started doing a do-si-do in the middle of the song 'Hair.' It was a sweet little moment." The show also came to serve as a farewell of sorts to Ragni, who died of cancer in 1991.

The UN performances served as a kind of template for many of the stagings that would follow. The show's instantly recognizable score and skimpy book made it a natural for minimally staged concert versions, among them a starry one-night benefit on Broadway in 2004 that featured Raúl Esparza, Jennifer Hudson, Gavin Creel, and, in a memorable basso profundo rendition of "Air," Harvey Fierstein. New York's Encores! series, which has transferred *Wonderful Town* and the long-running *Chicago* revival to Broadway, produced *HAIR* in 2001, and Los Angeles's similar Reprise! series followed suit a month later. For a brief period, both of these versions were circling Broadway: MacDermot, who had played keyboards for the Encores! shows, was partial to that production, while Rado leaned toward the Reprise! version. But despite one producer's attempt to somehow combine the two productions, the project ultimately foundered. It wasn't until six years later that another concert staging—one with an irresistible symmetry—put *HAIR* back on track to Broadway.

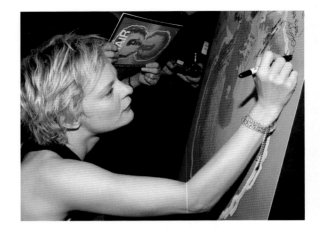

TOP Martha Plimpton, at a *HAIR* reunion in 2005, signs a poster of the show that introduced her parents to each other.

ABOVE Keith Carradine, Plimpton's father and a replacement Claude on Broadway, with the role's creator, James Rado, at the 2005 reunion.

RIGHT An open-air production of *HAIR* in Germany in 2006.

THE PUBLIC GETS INVOLVED

O skar Eustis was a disaffected 14-year-old—and not much of a theater buff—when he hitchhiked across Europe in 1972. Much as Michael Butler chanced upon the Public Theater, which Eustis would one day run, the teenage Eustis attended the London production of *HAIR* more or less on a whim. It changed his life.

"I danced on that stage, and I had a sense that there was a place for me in that tribe and, by that extension, a place for me in my country," says Eustis, who went on to become a prominent director and was named the fourth artistic director of the Public Theater in 2005. (He replaced George C. Wolfe, whose 12-year run as artistic director came after Joseph Papp's hand-picked successor, Joanne Akalaitis, lasted only 20 months.) "It helped create an image for me of what the theater could do."

The first show under Eustis's Public tenure was a revival of *Two Gentlemen of Verona* at Central Park's Delacorte Theater, better known as the home of Shakespeare in the Park, and he quickly hit it off with Galt MacDermot. Eustis had been trying to revive *HAIR* for almost a decade, dating back to his tenure as the artistic director of Trinity Rep in Providence, Rhode Island, but obtaining the rights was an issue. Rado was trying to mount his own revival on Broadway during this time, and Eustis broached the idea of an all-new script, which Rado quickly vetoed. "I think a lot of people have tried to revive *HAIR* without believing in its message or understanding it," Eustis says, "and Jim doesn't suffer those people. For good reason."

Finally, in late 2006, the pending fortieth anniversary of the Public Theater—as well as of the "American Tribal Love-Rock Musical" that inaugurated the theater—prompted Eustis to schedule a three-performance concert in the Delacorte for the following summer, with MacDermot himself on keyboards. For his creative team, Eustis hired the director Diane Paulus—whose 1999 hit *The Donkey Show* reset *A Midsummer Night's Dream* in a disco-era nightclub not unlike Cheetah—and the acclaimed modern-dance choreographer Karole Armitage.

The concert, nude scene and all, came together incredibly fast: Armitage says she staged the entire first act in one day. "It was nine days of Access Your Inner Hippie and done," Paulus says. Jonathan Groff, fresh from starring in the acclaimed rock musical *Spring Awakening*, played Claude and Will Swenson played Berger. The response was overwhelmingly positive, and Eustis immediately began plans to bring it back to the Delacorte the following summer as a fully-fledged production. "I have rarely felt forced to do a show," he says. "After those three days of concerts, I felt forced to do *HAIR*."

Once the adrenaline rush of the concerts had faded, Paulus settled in for immersion into all things *HAIR* with James Rado. "I sat with Jim for about six months," she says. "I got such a brain dump on *HAIR*." With the permission of

ABOVE Andrew Hamingson and Oskar Eustis attend the opening night of the Broadway revival of *HAIR* on March 31, 2009. Hamingson was named executive director of the Public Theater in 2008.

TOP RIGHT A three-night concert version was produced in Central Park in 2007 to commemorate the fortieth anniversary both of the Public and of *HAIR*.

BOTTOM RIGHT Galt MacDermot leads the onstage band (which includes his son Vince on trombone) at the 2007 concert.

LEFT The draft-card-burning scene at the anniversary concert. A few lines were added to the dialogue to explain how dangerous burning a draft card was in the 1960s.

ABOVE The ending of "Black Boys/White Boys" at the anniversary concert.

BELOW Will Swenson first played Berger at the anniversary concert.

Gerome Ragni's son, Erick, the two restored lines from the 1967 Public Theater production to the script and also added some exposition to make clear just how risky burning one's draft card was at the time.

Another nod to the 1967 production involved streamlining the scenes with the parents and other authority figures. Gerald Freedman had staged these with a pair of older actors who stood apart from the tribe; Tom O'Horgan fractured these scenes by casting six tribe members as a pair of (often cross-dressing) trios. Paulus, with Rado's help, settled on a comfortable and somewhat more realistic medium: The grown-ups are still played by members of the tribe, but only one at a time. "I thought that was a fresh idea," Rado says. "Those scenes with the three can be awfully funny but can be awfully awful, too."

The casting process in 2007 was as protracted as the rehearsals were brief: Paulus, Rado, and MacDermot spent months finding just the right tribe. Their efforts paid off in terms of longevity: All but three of the 26 performers from the 2007 concerts went on to Broadway. Each of the three versions had its own Sheila, however, and Groff left the show near the end of the 2008 Delacorte run. He was replaced on Broadway by Gavin Creel, who had played a tribe member in the 2001 Encores! production and sang "Going Down" at the 2004 benefit.

One point that Paulus insisted on pertained to the year of the show's setting. For the first two years, the world of *HAIR* aged along with its inhabitants: The Public and Cheetah productions were set in the autumn and winter of 1967, while the Broadway production reflected the fact that it opened in 1968. Since then, 1968 has been the play's setting, with the exception of the three-night concert that Diane Paulus directed in Central Park in 2007 which set it in 1967; Paulus half-jokingly posits that this was for the sake of fortieth anniversary publicity. (Sure

ABOVE James Rado, Galt MacDermot, and Diane Paulus during rehearsals in Central Park.

TOP RIGHT Another scene from the Central Park concert.

RIGHT TOP AND BOTTOM These performances in Central Park, like so many before them, would end with audience members joining the actors on stage (bottom right).

SODOMY

Sodomy
Fellatio
Cunnilingus
Pederasty

Father, why do these words sound
so nasty?

Masturbation
Can be fun
Join the holy orgy
Kama Sutra
Everyone!

"Sodomy"

We meet Woof, a conflicted Catholic who ponders why certain sexual descriptions have such potency.

JAMES RADO: *"These songs bring drugs and religion into the same space because they both offer a sort of liberation or transcendence."*

BRYCE RYNESS (Woof in 2009): *"It's essentially a deconstruction of these linguistic boogeymen that we have. 'Why do these words sound so nasty?' is a legitimate question."*

enough, when the full staging happened in Central Park the following year, the setting had shifted back to 1968.)

But when Paulus agreed to direct the production for Broadway, she and Rado both insisted that the setting be restored to 1967, just after the Summer of Love, which they viewed as a sort of prelapsarian age. The highest number of U.S. casualties in Vietnam came in 1968, with 1969 coming in second. 1967 was the year of Allen Ginsberg attempting to levitate the Pentagon and *Sgt. Pepper's Lonely Hearts Club Band*; 1968 was the year assassins' bullets ended the lives of Martin Luther King and Robert F. Kennedy, the year of the My Lai massacre in Vietnam and the Catonsville Nine in Maryland, the year of riots at the Democratic convention in Chicago and at Columbia University. (The Columbia riots had entered their seventh day the night *HAIR* opened at the Biltmore, less than four miles away, and would be violently quashed just a few hours later.)

The most important part of keeping this production alive, Paulus says, is making sure the actors don't move beyond what she calls "the possibility, the not knowing" of life in that era. "I went back recently and told them they were playing it like it was '70. It was, 'Been there, done that, fuck you,' as opposed to '67, which is, 'Everything is possible. And we are going to convert you from this stage tonight.'"

Everything, however, suddenly seemed impossible from a financial standpoint just as *HAIR* was beginning to make its case for a Broadway transfer. "Lehman collapsed the day after we closed in the Park," Eustis says, referring to the storied investment bank that came to symbolize the financial collapse of 2008. Despite terrific reviews—"Today *HAIR* seems, if anything, more daring than ever," wrote *Time* magazine's Richard Zoglin—finding investors able (or at least willing) to invest hundreds of thousands of dollars in a musical whose last Broadway revival was a complete failure became considerably more difficult. Announced Broadway revivals of such kindred shows as *Godspell* and Ntozake Shange's *For Colored Girls Who Have Considered Suicide When the Rainbow is Enuf* began to fall by the wayside.

Eustis's efforts began to compare with the zeal Michael Butler had lavished on *HAIR* for decades, as he attacked the prospective transfer with a verve that struck many at the time as quixotic. Not long after talking to the press about an arrangement whereby the theater would retain artistic control (and a healthy chunk of the profits) even though "not a dime of the Public's money is at

LEFT MacDermot and Rado attend rehearsals for the Broadway transfer of the Central Park production.

RIGHT Ronnie Dyson and Walter Michael Harris perform "What a Piece of Work Is Man" in 1968.

WHAT A PIECE OF WORK IS MAN

What a piece of work is man
How noble in reason
How infinite in faculties
In form and moving
How express and admirable
In action how like an angel
In apprehension how like a god
The beauty of the world
The paragon of animals

I have of late
But wherefore I know not
Lost all my mirth
This goodly frame
The earth
Seems to me a sterile promontory
This most excellent canopy
The air— look you!
This brave o'erhanging firmament
This majestical roof
Fretted with golden fire
Why it appears no other thing to me
Than a foul and pestilent congregation
Of vapors

What a piece of work is man
How noble in reason

How dare they try to end this beauty?
How dare they try to end this beauty?

Walking in space
We find the purpose of peace
The beauty of life
You can no longer hide

Our eyes are open
Our eyes are open
Our eyes are open
Our eyes are open
Wide wide wide!

LEFT Rado, Paulus, and MacDermot at the 2009 Broadway premier.

BELOW Bryce Ryness (left) and other tribe members celebrate opening night at the Al Hirschfeld Theater.

RIGHT TOP AND BOTTOM The curtain call at opening night included original cast members Melba Moore and Rado (top, at center.)

risk," Eustis found himself in the position of having to nudge his lead producer, Elizabeth I. McCann, off to the side and bring in additional producers—without losing McCann's investors in the process. This generated far less welcome attention in the press; admitting that your principal investor couldn't raise the needed cash and is threatening to sue did not speak well for the show's prospects. The widely read *New York Post* gossip columnist Michael Riedel quoted one theater insider as saying, "Oskar's in the hot seat. He'd better hope *HAIR* is a hit."

It was. *HAIR* opened on March 31, 2009, at the recently renamed Al Hirschfeld Theater, and the reviews were rapturous—better than the original production had received in either of its iterations. "*HAIR* is a musical for the ages because it is a musical for the now," wrote Elisabeth Vincentelli of the *New York Post,* while *The New York Times's* Ben Brantley lavished particular praise on the direction: "It's not so much what Ms. Paulus brings to *HAIR*, it's what she brings out of it, vital elements that were always waiting to be rediscovered." The box office numbers rose accordingly, and *HAIR* would ultimately recoup its $5.76 million investment in less than five months. In 1968, Mayor John Lindsay was fielding calls to close the show and/or arrest the actors; in March 2010, the new mayor, Mike Bloomberg, appeared in hippie garb and sang several reworked *HAIR* lyrics alongside cast members at a charity dinner.

While nearly everyone involved with the original production was happy for the revival's success (it completed its run on June 27, after 519 performances), many of them questioned whether the current cast members, none of whom was alive

LEFT As with the original, "Frank Mills" (performed here by Allison Case on *Good Morning America*) proved to be a popular song at television appearances.

BELOW Gavin Creel (center) and Will Swenson perform the title song on *Good Morning America.*

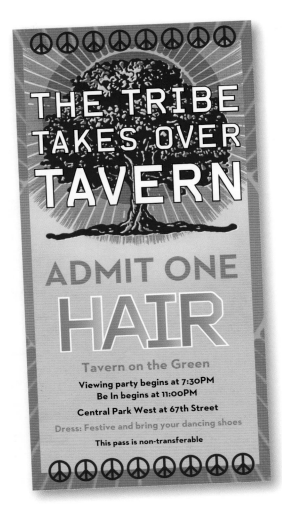

when *HAIR* first opened on Broadway, truly conveyed the sense of inhabiting that era. This criticism has dogged the show from the very beginning: Gerald Freedman and several critics feel the Tom O'Horgan production took a similarly glib approach to the material. Indeed, the fear of estheticizing and therefore defanging the hippie movement was there in that very first production. Remember the taunting announcer at the original Be-In: "Tourists. See the Hippies... Watch safely through our shatterproof sky dome bus-o-rama. See, see, see the Hippie Phenomenon."

In any event, the Broadway establishment did not appear to share this sentiment. By 2009, *HAIR* was safely entrenched in the Broadway canon, and that year's Tony Awards reflected this comfort. The revival received eight nominations—six more than the original, presumably more threatening production—and won the award for Best Revival of a Musical. In so doing, *HAIR* became the only musical in history to win Best Revival after being shut out completely in its original incarnation. (Among the shows it beat out was *West Side Story*. Karen Olivo, who won a Tony for her portrayal of Anita in that show, played Sheila Franklin in the three 2007 Delacorte concerts of *HAIR*.)

When he accepted the award on behalf of a jubilant tribe, Eustis used the platform to paraphrase one of the slogans from *HAIR*—but not to address the environment or the war or any of the other hot-button topics that the show confronts. "Peace now, freedom now, *equality* now," he said, grabbing his own wedding ring as he emphasized the third noun in a clear reference to the movement toward legal recognition of same-sex marriage (Eustis is married to a woman). This heartfelt speech signaled a new outlet for the humanism that *HAIR* has advocated and inspired for almost 45 years. He and his cast would soon make good on Eustis's pledge in a very public way.

ABOVE A ticket for the Tony Awards party sponsored by *HAIR*, complete with post-awards "Be In."

LEFT The cast, led by Sasha Allen, performs on *Late Show With David Letterman*.

RIGHT The Broadway cast at the 2009 Tony Awards, where the show fared better than it had at the 1969 awards.

THE SOCIAL MESSAGE CONTINUES

Broadway performers don't sacrifice their days off lightly. Particularly when the show they're in requires that they be on stage constantly (except when they're in the audience.) Particularly when a rejigged schedule means they have just done 16 consecutive shows. Particularly when the "day" in question begins at 11 p.m. the night before, as they pile onto a bus immediately after the sixteenth show. But October 11, 2009, saw almost the entire cast of *HAIR* do just that, arriving in Washington, D.C. a little before dawn and preparing to perform as part of the National Equality March.

They were there at the behest of the *HAIR* star Gavin Creel, who had been fairly apolitical until Election Night 2008. Like many other gay men, Creel seesawed between conflicting emotions that night: His elation at Barack Obama's victory was tempered by the passage of Proposition 8, a statewide referendum in California that banned same-sex marriage. Also, like many other gay men and women, especially those who live outside California, he found it hard to know how to channel his anger. First he helped to create Broadway Impact, an organization dedicated to generating support for the cause within the theater community.

An additional opportunity presented itself in May 2009 at the CD release party of the *HAIR* cast recording, when he met the prominent gay activist Cleve Jones. Best known as the creator of the AIDS Memorial Quilt and a close friend of the San Francisco gay rights leader Harvey Milk, Jones was organizing the Washington march, which was advocating gay marriage rights. The two hit it off, and Creel immediately sought out Oskar Eustis to suggest that the *HAIR* cast participate in the march.

Eustis consulted with the show's general manager that same night and began to work out the logistics of canceling the *HAIR* matinee that was scheduled for the day of the march. It was quickly decided that the cost, while not insubstantial, would not be ruinous and that a substitute performance could be scheduled for the Monday before (which resulted in the 16 consecutive shows). Before long, among the peace signs brandished during the curtain-call dance were ones that said, "Our tribe is going. Are you?"

"I think the marriage equality movement stemmed from two situations," says cast member Bryce Ryness, who carried a "With Liberty and Justice for All" sign at the march. "One, Gavin has a great platform, and this is something that kept him up at night. And two, Oskar really believed in making this show a geopolitical event. It almost didn't matter to him what cause we found, just as long as he knew it was killing us, whatever it was."

This level of idealism is what prompted Cameron Mackintosh to import virtually the entire Broadway company (all but six of the 26 original cast members) to London for the West End revival, which premiered on April 1, 2010, at the Gielgud Theatre. Mackintosh, who worked backstage on the original

ABOVE Galt MacDermot at his Staten Island home in 2001. His post-*HAIR* compositions have been sampled by everyone from Public Enemy to Busta Rhymes to Snoop Dogg.

LEFT James Rado continues to tinker with the book of *HAIR* as well as work on his next musical, *A Cool Soldier*.

RIGHT The Broadway cast attends an Equality Now media event in Los Angeles in July 2009.

LEFT Cast members pose with Speaker of the House Nancy Pelosi (center) and her husband, Paul Pelosi (far left,) backstage after a performance.

BELOW LEFT The tribe wore considerably more clothes than usual when it kicked off 2010 at the Times Square New Year's Eve celebration.

London production while in his early twenties—"the show *marked* him," Diane Paulus says—felt that Britain's young actors were too jaded to take on the show until they had seen the Americans do it for six months. Ultimately, however, the production fell short of the six-month mark by a few weeks, closing on September 4.

Many people who marched with the *HAIR* company in Washington say they were grateful for the chance to join the sort of cause their hippie predecessors might have embraced. History was on the mind of Jonathan Groff, who joined his former cast members, when he described the scene to a reporter: "This is what the pictures in every history book we read to research *HAIR* looked like. And now we're all here."

Indeed, in letting the message of *HAIR* spill beyond the theater and into a dismayingly unforgiving outer world, these young men and women were forging a link to the roiling, exhilarating, punishing era that left such an imprint on James Rado and Gerome Ragni. "There are very few shows that reflected the time and also changed it," says Natalie Mosco, "and *HAIR* is one of them."

Walter Michael Harris is a perfect example of this. "I went into *HAIR* as an actor and left as a hippie," he says. Harris's older brother George, who had renamed himself Hibiscus, had already moved from New York to a commune in San Francisco, stopping along the way at another demonstration in Washington, D.C. It was here that Hibiscus put carnations into the gun barrels of U.S. troops guarding the Pentagon; Bernie Boston's photograph of this intervention became an iconic image of the hippie movement, one that Paulus replicated in her *HAIR* staging.

"The core values of *HAIR* became my core values," Harris says. "It's a celebration of the human family and an earnest plea for the end of war, for harmony and understanding and peace." In the summer of 1969, he left the *HAIR* company and joined Hibiscus at the commune.

This impulse toward activism and generosity has consistently fueled the casts of *HAIR* in productions large and small. Gerome Ragni and James Rado supplied the show's ever-mutating DNA; Galt MacDermot gave it a pulse; Gerald

RIGHT Forty years after it played to sold-out theaters, *HAIR* returned to Belgrade (now the capital of Serbia) in early 2010.

Freedman (with Anna Sokolow as an all-but-silent partner) provided a spine; Michael Butler nudged it into existence with a blend of fanaticism and savvy; and Tom O'Horgan and Julie Arenal saw to it that this loud, ungainly, vibrant creation grew into the phenomenon it is today. However, it owes its longevity to the tens of thousands of performers who have continually breathed cantankerous, blissful life into it.

Few of these men and women ended up at a commune like Walter Michael Harris. All the same, *HAIR* leaves an indelible impression on nearly everyone who performs in it, each chipping away at an increasingly commodified society until their own bit of sun shines in. Nina Machlin Dayton, whose work on behalf of the *HAIR* archives has put her in contact with hundreds of actors, directors, and designers, says she tells each cast at the beginning of rehearsals, "I guarantee you will be changed by doing this show." She invariably checks in with each of them after the production has opened. She has yet to be wrong.

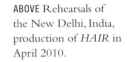

ABOVE Rehearsals of the New Delhi, India, production of *HAIR* in April 2010.

LEFT Sasha Allen and the cast of the Broadway revival perform "Aquarius" at London's Gielgud Theatre, also in April 2010.

RIGHT There ain't no words for the beauty, the splendor, the wonder of *HAIR*.

INDEX

Page numbers in *italic* type refer to illustrations or their captions.

CREDITS & ACKNOWLEDGMENTS

Author's Acknowledgments

Thank you to the following interview subjects: Sargent Aborn, Julie Arenal, Karole Armitage, Michael Butler, Robert Camuto, Mary Lorrie Davis, Nina Machlin Dayton, Linda Compton Davis, Sally Eaton, Jules Fisher, Gerald Freedman, Merle Frimark, Bernard Gersten, Jenny Gersten, William Goldman, Linda Greenhouse, Walter Michael Harris, Marjorie Lipari, James Lovell, Galt MacDermot, Natalie Mosco, Darius Nichols, Diane Paulus, Amy Louise Pommier, James Rado, Robert I. Rubinsky, Bryce Ryness, Amy Saltz, Daniel Sullivan, Will Swenson, Dr. William Swiggard.

Special thanks to: Linda Buchwald, Bill Glavin, Jesse Green, Mike Greenwald, Brigid Grode, George Grode, John Guiton, Dr. Elizabeth Harre, Ken Mandelbaum, John Pike, Stephen Sondheim, Elizabeth Wagner, Jonathan Wells, the kind and patient staff of Palombo Bakery.

Picture Credits

The publishers would like to thank the following sources for their kind permission to reproduce the pictures in this book. The page numbers for each of the photographs are listed below, giving the page on which they appear in the book.

Image location indicator: (t=top, b=bottom, l=left, c=center, r=right)

© **Corbis: Bettmann:** 10 (t), 10 (bl), 11, 25 (t), 25 (b), 44, 45, 54 (b), 86 (b), 111 (t); /Allen Ginsberg: 13; /Hulton-Deutsch Collection: 10 (cr); /Flip Schulke: 108 © **Michael Butler:** 41 (b), 43 (tl), 43 (tr), 43 (b), 46, 49, 67, 74, 74, 74, 74, 78 (t), 94 (b), 95, 96 (bl), 96 (br), 100 (t), 105 (t), 113, 120 © **Dagmar/www.dagmarfoto.com:** 2, 4, 5 (b), 7 (t), 7 (b), 9 (photo 1, 4, 5 and 7), 14 (b), 18, 22 (t), 22 (b), 24, 26 (t), 29 (t), 29 (b), 30 (t), 30 (c), 31, 32, 33, 34 (t), 34 (b), 35, 36, 37 (t), 37 (b), 39, 40 (t), 40 (b), 41 (t), 42 (t), 47, 48, 50 (t), 50 (c), 51, 52, 53, 54 (t), 55, 56, 57, 58 (t), 58 (c), 60, 62 (t), 62 (c), 62 (b), 64, 66, 68, 69, 70, 71, 72 (t), 72 (b), 73 (t), 74 (t), 74 (c), 76, 81, 86 (t), 87, 88 (t), 88 (b), 90, 91, 93, 100 (c), 100 (b), 101, 102 (t), 102 (b), 103, 118 (l), 118 (r), 119, 121, 122, 123 (b), 124 (t), 124 (b), 127 (b), 130 (r), 133, 142, 150 (t), 150 (b) © **Getty Images:** 12, 15, 19, 20, 42 (b), 65, 77, 80, 83, 84 (t), 84 (c), 92, 94 (t), 96 (t), 114, 115, 116, 130 (l), 131 (t), 132 (t), 132 (c), 134 (t), 134 (c), 136, 139, 144 (b), 145 (t), 145 (b), 146, 147, 151, 152 (t), 152 (b), 153, 154 (t); /National Geographic: 107; /Popperfoto: 16; /Time & Life Pictures: 14, 23, 26 (c); /Wireimage: 144 (t) © **Lebrecht Photo Library:** 89; **/NYPL Performing Arts:** 59; /RA: 105 (b), 106 © **Joan Marcus:** 9 (photo 6), 27, 123 (c), 137 (t), 137 (b), 138, 139 (t), 140 (l), 140 (r), 141 (t), 141 (b) © **N.A.S.A.:** 11 (b) © **Chase Newhart:** 8, 9 (photo 2, 3 and 8), 63, 110 **Courtesy of Diane Paulus:** 6 © **Press Association Images:** 142, 148, 149 (b) **Private Collection:** 112 © **The Public Theater:** 149 (t) **Courtesy of James Rado:** 38 © **Rex Features: Alinari:** 73; /Daily Sketch: 99; /Everett Collection: 117, 126, 127 (t); /Geraint Lewis: 155; /Alistair Muir: 154 (b) **Courtesy of the Sokolow Dance Foundation:** 26 (cr) © **Topfoto.co.uk:** 99 (t), 129, 130 (t), 131 (bl), 131 (br); /Arena/PAL: 98; /Spectrum/HIP: 97; /Ullstein Bild: 104 (t), 104 (b), 134 © **U.S. Games Systems:** 5 (t)

Every effort has been made to acknowledge correctly and contact the source and/copyright holder of each picture, and Carlton Books Limited apologises for any unintentional errors or omissions, which will be corrected in further editions of this book.

Publisher's Acknowledgments

The publishers would like to thank the following people for their assistance in the production of this book: Michael Butler, Nina Dayton at The Hair Archives, Dagmar, Cristal Mackenzie, Adam Dixon, Eric Louie, Jenny Gersten, Derek Zasky

Editorial Director: Piers Murray Hill
Editorial Manager: Vanessa Daubney
Commissioning Editor : Jonathan Wells
Executive Editor: Jennifer Barr
Copy-editor: Stella Caldwell
Additional editorial work: Catherine Rubinstein,
    Alice Payne, Gemma Maclagan, Nicky Jeanes, Anne Barrett
Creative Director: Clare Baggaley
Art Editor: Sooky Choi
Design: Sally Bond
Additional design work: Darren Jordan
Picture Manager: Steve Behan
Production Manager: Rachel Burgess

FURTHER INFORMATION

Archives

The HAIR Archives holds material on the history of the show from its inception up to current productions, The HAIR Archives, 44 School Street, Hatfield, MA 01038, http://www.orlok.com/hair/

Some of Michael Butler's papers are kept at the Mugar Memorial Library, Boston University, 771 Commonwealth Avenue, Boston, MA 02215, United States, http://www.bu.edu/library/mugar/index.shtml

Papers belonging to Joseph Papp and Gerome Ragni can be found in The New York Public Library for the Performing Arts, Dorothy and Lewis B. Cullman Center, 40 Lincoln Center Plaza New York, NY 10023-7498, United States, http://www.nypl.org/

Websites

www.hairthemusical.com
http://www.orlok.com/hair/holding/Hair.html
http://www.michaelbutler.com/blog/hair/

Books

"*Letting Down My HAIR: Two Years With the Love Rock Tribe—From the Dawning to the Downing of Aquarius*" by Lorrie Davis and Rachel Gallagher, A. Fields Books, 1973.

"*Good HAIR Days: A Personal Journey With the American Tribal Love-Rock Musical HAIR*" by Jonathon Johnson, iUniverse, Inc., 2004.

"*The Age of HAIR: Evolution and Import of Broadway's First Rock Musical*" by Barbara Lee Horn, Greenwood Press, 1991.

"*Let the Sun Shine In: The Genius of HAIR*" by Scott Miller, Heinmann, 2003.

MICHAEL BUTLER PRESENTS

HAIR

THE AMERICAN TRIBAL LOVE-ROCK MUSICAL

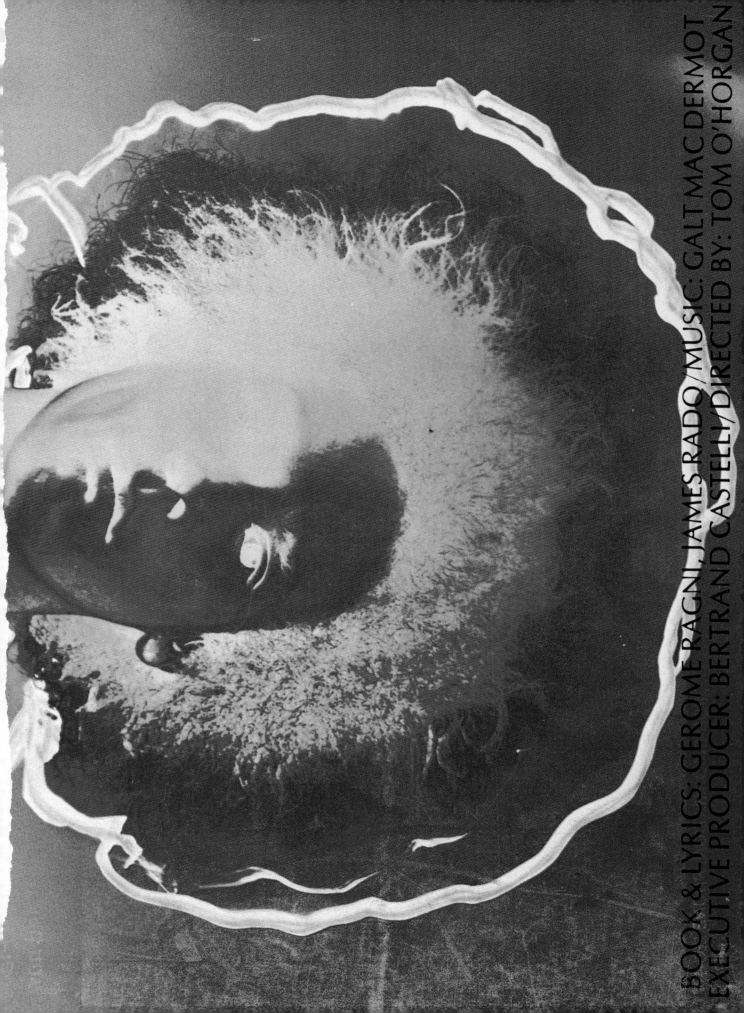

BOOK & LYRICS: GEROME RAGNI, JAMES RADO/MUSIC: GALT MAC DERMOT
EXECUTIVE PRODUCER: BERTRAND CASTELLI/DIRECTED BY: TOM O'HORGAN